EL RINOCERONTE II

Rinocerología Avanzada

"Para ayudarte a través de la jungla"

EL RINOCERONTE II
RINOCEROLOGÍA AVANZADA

Por Scott Alexander

Ilustraciones de Laurie Smallwood

EDICIONES
BOTAS

Título original:
Advanced Rhinocerology
© 1981, by Scott Robert Alexander

Traducción: Gabriela Botas
Tipografía: Bolita Design Studio

Derechos Reservados:

© **Librería y Ediciones Botas S.A. de C.V.**
Justo Sierra 52, Col. Centro.
C.P. 06020, México D.F.
Tels.   702-4083 y 702-5403
Fax   702-5403

ISBN: 968-6334-21-1

Prohibida la reproducción parcial o total por cualquier medio, ya sea electrónico, óptico o mecánico, sin la autorización expresa del editor.

CONTENIDO

Capítulo	Página
DEDICATORIA	7
ADVERTENCIA	9
INTRODUCCIÓN	11
1. NO SEAS UNA VACA	13
2. HAY UNA JUNGLA ALLÁ AFUERA	21
3. CONOCE A TU GUÍA PARA EL SAFARI	31
4. LA CACERÍA	35
5. RENUNCIA A TU EMPLEO	43
6. EL MIEDO A SER APLASTADO	59
7. EL JUEGO DE LA LIBRE EMPRESA	69
8. UN SAFARI EMPRESARIAL	85
9. LA REVOLUCIÓN RINOCERÓNTICA	91
10. EDUCACIÓN DE LA JUNGLA	107
11. EPÍLOGO	121

DEDICADO A:

Bob y Cynthia Alexander
L.J. Howard
Dr. Robert y Mary Lou Landes
Shylie Lewis
Paul, Karen y Heather Teague

¡¡¡ADVERTENCIA!!!

¡Se aconseja que la información contenida en este libro sea SÓLO leída por rinocerontes! Si por ahora eres una vaca, NO sigas leyendo. ¡ESTA PROHIBIDO! (Estás transgrediendo una ley). Por favor, repórtate en tu pastura y que tengas una buena ruina.

Gracias por tu cooperación.

INTRODUCCIÓN

Tu respiración se llena con un olor bochornoso, fuerte y sofocante mientras tus fosas nasales se ensanchan, expulsando el aire de tus grandes pulmones. En cuestión de horas, a veces minutos, has aumentado 2,500 kilogramos... espero que distribuidos en los lugares correctos. Tu piel se ensancha y se torna de 5 centímetros de espesor. Un cuerno empieza a crecer justo en tu frente mientras los músculos de tus piernas empiezan a crisparse debido al exceso de energía que corre por tu cuerpo. De repente, sientes el impulso de dejar salir tu primer gruñido de rinoceronte. Un fuerte rugido viene bramando desde lo más profundo de tu ser y sales a la carga. ¡Otro rinoceronte encuentra su camino a la jungla!

Desde la presentación de "El Rinoceronte" en 1980, miles se han convertido en rinocerontes o, por primera vez, se dieron cuenta de que ya eran rinos. La década de los rinocerontes llegó. La realización, la prosperidad y, sobre todo, la felicidad, son las características del rino. SÍ, ES una jungla allá afuera, pero tú estás listo para la aventura de todos modos, ¿o no? ¡Afilen sus cuernos y vamos a la carga!

Capítulo 1

NO SEAS UNA VACA

Si estás buscando una manera fácil de triunfar, de ser feliz, de hacerte rico, o de lograr cualquier cosa, entonces este libro no es para ti. Deja de buscar. No hay caminos fáciles para llegar el éxito. Una vida de aventura, de logros y de felicidad no es para los flojos de piel delgada.

El éxito es éxito porque es difícil lograrlo. Decir que el éxito es fácil es sólo quitarles mérito a aquéllos que han triunfado. Si llegar a triunfar fuera fácil, si cualquiera pudiera hacerlo, no sería un triunfo, ¿o sí? ¡Sería mediocridad!

Ser mediocre es fácil. Es por eso que hay tanta gente con vidas mediocres. Viven su vida pastando, siguiéndose unos a otros, día tras día, año tras año, quejándose y racionalizando su miserable existencia. Las vacas tienden a aplazarlo todo y nunca logran nada en toda su vida.

LAS VACAS SON MISERABLES

Esa no es la forma más deseable de pasar el poco tiempo que tienes aquí en la tierra. La vida es una aventura, y una aventura debe ser divertida,

¿correcto? Las vacas simplemente no se divierten. ¿Alguna vez has visto a una vaca sonreír? Las vacas no sonríen. ¡También les cuesta trabajo reírse! Estoy seguro de que ya has visto algunas. El gobierno contrata muchas vacas para trabajar en el departamento de tránsito. ¡Qué forma tan miserable de vivir! Por supuesto, yo tampoco serviría si fuera una vaca. El día más emocionante para las vacas es cuando son llevadas al matadero.

LOS RINOS SON FELICES

Por otra parte hay gente que está haciendo de todo. ¡Ellos son rinocerontes! Los rinos son los que están creando sus propios negocios, comprando y vendiendo bienes raíces, viajando por todo el mundo, criando familias felices, pasando sus vidas haciendo lo que les gusta hacer y viviendo vidas de aventuras, cargando por doquier en la jungla.

¡Y sí *es* una jungla allá afuera! ¡Sólo observa las noticias de las diez y te darás cuenta de la jungla que es! Afortunadamente, no es tan malo como la televisión y los periódicos te lo pintan. ¡Pero ciertamente hay determinados peligros y eso es lo que la hace una aventura!

Las aventuras son divertidas porque siempre hay ese elemento de riesgo, la intriga y el suspenso de lo desconocido. A veces te atorarás en el lodo. Simplemente acéptalo como parte de la emoción y busca la forma de salir en vez de darte por vencido y hundirte como una vaca lo haría. ¡Tú eres un rinoceronte! ¡Amas la aventura! Nunca te verás pastando sin rumbo en una pastura y buscando un lugar para echarte.

¡Los rinocerontes son cargadores! Es por eso que los rinos son famosos por: cargar, actuar, moverse y estar llenos de energía. Una vez que tengas el espíritu rinoceronte de *me importa un comino*, una vez que empieces a tomar acción inmediata cada día, ya estás en camino hacia donde sea que quieras llegar.

LA ACCIÓN ES ESENCIAL

Hay muchos libros que apoyan el hábito de escribir tus metas después de visualizar tu camino hacia el éxito, y no creo que puedas sentarte en tu casa y visualizar tu camino hacia el éxito. ¡Ese es un cuento de hadas para vacas! ¡Un nuevo Rolls-Royce no llegará a tocar a tu puerta sólo porque te quedaste en tu casa y lo visualizaste tres veces al día! Eso va contra las leyes de la naturaleza.

YO SÍ creo que visualizar el Rolls-Royce y después actuar para conseguirlo algún día hará que el empleado de la agencia llegue hasta tu puerta a entregarte las llaves. ¡Pero otra vez; la clave más importante es CARGAR, y no quiero decir cargar a tu cuenta de tarjeta de crédito! Ten cuidado con las abejas asesinas... los bancos. Si te metes en problemas, ¡ve a que te hagan "cirugía plástica" y que te extraigan las tarjetas de crédito!.

"¡Es divertido ser un rinoceronte!"

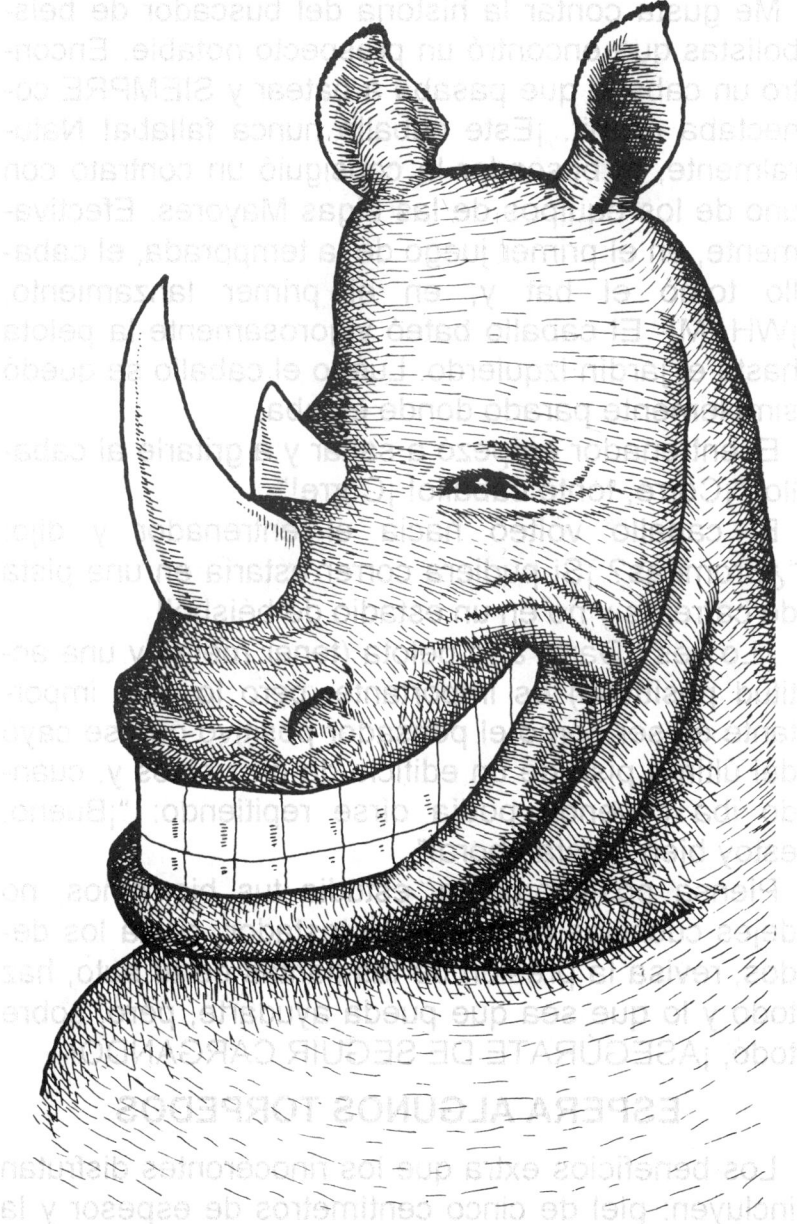

Me gusta contar la historia del buscador de beisbolistas que encontró un prospecto notable. Encontró un caballo que pasaba a batear y SIEMPRE conectaba un hit. ¡Este caballo nunca fallaba! Naturalmente, el buscador le consiguió un contrato con uno de los equipos de las Ligas Mayores. Efectivamente, en el primer juego de la temporada, el caballo tomó el bat y, en el primer lanzamiento, ¡WHAM!- El caballo bateó vigorosamente la pelota hasta el jardín izquierdo. Luego el caballo se quedó simplemente parado donde estaba.

El entrenador empezó a saltar y a gritarle al caballo: "¡Corre, tonto caballo! ¡Corre!"

El caballo volteó hacia el entrenador y dijo: "¿Bromeas? ¡Si pudiera correr estaría en una pista de carreras y no en un estadio de béisbol!

¿Lo ves? Darle a la pelota (tener metas y una actitud positivas) es importante, pero lo más importante es ser como el pensador positivo que se cayó del último piso de un edificio de diez pisos y, cuando iba cayendo podía oírse repitiendo: "¡Bueno, estoy bien, hasta ahora!"

Piensa positivamente, estudia tus biorritmos, no dejes cuchillos dentro de tu tostador, cruza los dedos, revisa la presión de las llantas de tu auto, haz todo y lo que sea que pueda ayudarte, pero, sobre todo, ¡ASEGÚRATE DE SEGUIR CARGANDO!

ESPERA ALGUNOS TORPEDOS

Los beneficios extra que los rinocerontes disfrutan incluyen: piel de cinco centímetros de espesor y la audacia que los caracteriza. Con un espíritu rinoceronte de *me importan un comino los torpedos*, los rinocerontes son conocidos por atrapar la mayoría de los torpedos. Los torpedos son los problemas, las demoras, y el rechazo que enfrentamos cada día.

¡Oye! ¡Todo eso viene con el territorio! ¡La jungla no tiene bardas! ¡No hay seguridad! Ni siquiera las vacas están totalmente seguras echadas en su pastura. De vez en cuando, los torpedos pasan a través de sus cercas y terminan con un par de ellas. Ellas no tienen la piel de cinco centímetros de espesor como nosotros.

La mejor manera de engrosar tu cuero es exponerlo a los torpedos. Después de que te hayan golpeado algunas veces, tu piel comienza a endurecerse. Esto no significa que seas insensible a los demás. De hecho, los rinocerontes son conocidos por ser los animales más cariñosos, serviciales y generosos.

Los rinocerontes donan el dinero para construir hospitales y universidades. Construyen bibliotecas y parques, y todo lo que pueda contribuir al mejoramiento del mundo. Si hay alguien insensible a los demás, ésas son las vacas. Son improductivas y no contribuyen en nada. Las vacas quieren que se les cuide y nada les gustaría más que todo el mundo compartiera su apestosa pastura llena de estiércol. ¡Eso es ser insensible!

LA AUDACIA ES DIVERTIDA

Finalmente, tú eres audaz. Piensa en los jugadores de fútbol americano. ¿Crees que ellos se pondrían a golpearse unos a otros de esa manera si no tuvieran su cuerpo protegido con cojines y un casco en la cabeza? ¡De ninguna manera! Serían mucho más precavidos. Es su equipo protector lo que les permite jugar rudo.

Es lo mismo siendo un rinoceronte. Tu piel de cinco centímetros de espesor es tu equipo protector. ¡Es lo que te permite mandar a la cautela al demonio! Harás cosas audaces como invertir todo tu dinero en un nuevo negocio, o renunciar a tu empleo de 20 años para vender bienes raíces, o cualquier otra cosa que siempre has deseado hacer pero que no habías tenido las agallas o el temple para hacerlo. Recuerda, ¡la vida es una aventura! ¡Es divertido ser audaz!

Capítulo 2

HAY UNA JUNGLA ALLÁ AFUERA

¿Puedes sentir su premura? ¿Puedes sentir la emoción que la rudeza, la singularidad y la resonancia de la jungla generan? ¿Ves las oportunidades aquí? ¿Puedes oír los sonidos extraños, los chillidos, los gritos, los rugidos y la risa? Así es, la vida es una jungla.

¿El sofocante calor hace que tu sangre fluya más rápido? ¿El confuso bullicio de la actividad te anima? ¿Las largas, oscuras y frías noches te hacen sentir ansioso? Conforme la luz del sol matinal se filtra a través de los altos matorrales y la frondosa vegetación para iluminar un nuevo día ¿Sientes la urgencia de ser parte de todo eso?

La jungla está esperando.

Tu pulso se acelera y parece completar el aura de la jungla, latiendo con una fuerza intensa y rítmica que te marca como miembro de un mundo complejo y desordenado. Al aspirar el húmedo y terroso aire, tu mente da vueltas mientras observas el tamaño de todo lo que te rodea. ¿Puedes sentir la intensidad, la constante estimulación, y la satisfacción de saber dónde te encuentras? ¡Tú y la jungla ya son uno!

"Los rinos aman la jungla"

No hay nada como dramatizar un poco para transmitirte la idea, ¿cierto? ¿Lo sientes ahora? Hablando en serio, hay una jungla allá afuera, ¡pero esto es grandioso porque los rinos aman la jungla! Estamos armados para funcionar mejor en la jungla con nuestra piel gruesa, nuestra audacia, nuestra constancia y nuestra energía.

NADIE DIJO QUE SERÍA FÁCIL

Por supuesto que existen molestias y sufrimientos. *¡Nadie dijo que la jungla era justa!* Claro que hay peligros en la vida (Y en el limbo). La muerte, por inconveniente o desagradable que te parezca, sucede en la jungla TODO EL TIEMPO *¡Nadie dijo que sería seguro!* La vida en la jungla puede a veces ser tan frustrante que algunos en vez de esperar a que los maten, se matan a sí mismos. *¡Nadie dijo que sería fácil!*

Así que existen la pena y la crueldad, el dolor y la enfermedad, la muerte y destrucción, como sucesos diarios en la jungla. Pues bien, *¡nadie dijo que sería aburrido!* ¡Da gracias por esto! Está bien sentirte triste o enojado, puedes temblar de miedo, está permitido gritar de angustia, y no hay nada malo en estar muerto. Pero vivir una vida de aburrimiento es peor que simplemente no vivir gracias a la jungla. Tú nunca tendrás que vivir un destino peor que la misma muerte. Gracias a la jungla todo lo que tienes que hacer es abrir los ojos, todo lo que tienes que hacer es escuchar lo que sucede a tu alrededor, ¡y te garantizo que NUNCA estarás aburrido!

NUNCA SE PUEDE ASEGURAR NADA

Esta jungla en la que vivimos es todo menos aburrida. Hay muy pocas probabilidades de predecir lo que va a pasar. ¡De hecho, si hay algo de lo que puedes estar seguro, es de la imposibilidad que tienes de predecir algo! Crea tu propia empresa ¿y qué pasará? ¿quién lo sabe? Puedes volverte rico o quebrar totalmente. Ve a dar un paseo ¿y qué podría pasar? ¡No hay forma de saberlo! Puede que te encuentres con el animal más bello del bosque y tengas un gran romance salvaje o puede que te atropelle un camión. ¡De cualquier manera estás en problemas!

El simple hecho de poder tener tus ocho horas de sueño tiene cierta incertidumbre. Tal vez el viejo corazón de rino decidiera detenerse mientras estás lejos en el país de los sueños. Los corazones no trabajan por siempre, tú lo sabes. De vez en cuando se ponen en huelga.

¿Qué estarás haciendo en diez años? Puedes adivinar, puedes presuponer, puedes especular, pero nunca podrás estar seguro de nada. En diez años, podrías formar parte de una de las estadísticas más desafortunadas de la jungla, o podrías estar viviendo en el éxtasis. Podrías poseer vastas extensiones de tierras en la jungla y vivir en una increíble mansión con tu familia de rinos. Tener vacaciones periódicas a otras junglas, donde eres reconocido y respetado, sería una forma de pasar parte de tu tiempo. Podrías tener una vida de rino

"Podrías darte la gran vida de rino además de tus masajes de gruesa piel"

completa, con manicura diario en tu cuerno, masajes a tu gruesa piel, tu propia alberca de lodo en el patio trasero, un ejemplar de la primera edición de "Rinocerología avanzada" y un Rolls-Royce con tu nombre en la placa.

LA JUNGLA ES INJUSTA

¡Hay una jungla allá afuera y es emocionante! A veces parece que existe el mal y la obscuridad por necesidad, ya que por cada cosa buena hay una cosa mala, para cada ácido hay un alcalino, y por cada lágrima hay una risa. Así es, la bondad en realidad abunda en la jungla.

Nadie dijo que la jungla era justa y esto es correcto porque cuando la jungla se les dificulta a algunos, también permite a otros dar, lo que a su vez enriquece a todos. La desgracia de unos permite a otros apreciar y amar donde antes pudo haber existido indiferencia.

La injusticia de la jungla provoca una compasión y un interés tan profundos, que de otra forma no aflorarían. Provoca una piedad que, sin la flagrante ferocidad de la jungla, podría nunca despertar en alguna parte dentro de nuestras almas animales. Sólo la crueldad y la violencia de la jungla pueden sacar a flote las emociones de amor y paz, de dar y compartir, y la determinación de superar las injusticias de la jungla nos hace unirnos a todos ante las adversidades.

LA VIDA EN LA JUNGLA PUEDE SER PELIGROSA

Nadie dijo que estarías a salvo, lo cual, repito, es afortunado. Los peligros de la jungla nos hacen ser cautelosos y precavidos para que no actuemos con temeridad. Está bien atacar con un espíritu de "no me importan los torpedos", porque demasiada precaución puede ser perjudicial, pero, hagas lo que hagas, ¡NO te pares frente a los torpedos cuando los veas venir! Algunos de los torpedos más grandes pueden ser esquivados.

De hecho, en alguna parte de la jungla se encuentra el torpedo más grande que hayas visto con tu nombre escrito en él, ¡y ese es el que quieres evitar por tanto tiempo como sea posible! Sin embargo, no pierdas tu tiempo preocupándote e inquietándote por esto, o te expones a morirte de la angustia antes de que te llegue tu hora.

Es cierto, la muerte y la enfermedad van por la jungla desenfrenadamente, sin embargo, también abundan la vida y la felicidad. Además, tanto la muerte como la vida nos sirven para recordarnos que la jungla es sólo un safari temporal, mientras esperamos para estar con el Señor. Si la muerte sirve de algo, además de eventualmente matarte, debería llenarte de amor a Dios y de una confianza en Él tan fuerte que la muerte sea la menor de tus preocupaciones.

VIVIR EN LA JUNGLA ES UN DESAFÍO

Finalmente, nadie dijo que sería fácil, ya que con lo fácil viene la apatía y con la apatía viene el aburrimiento: *la muerte final.* Gracias a la jungla, la vida no es fácil. El mal es fácil. ¡Morir, engañar, perder o ser mediocre es FÁCIL! ¡Aléjate de lo fácil!
Lo bueno cuesta trabajo. Cualquier logro es un desafío. Tú eres tenaz, así que enfréntate a lo adverso. Acoge las situaciones difíciles para fortalecerte. Utiliza la incertidumbre para hacer tu fe más sólida. Válete de los obstáculos de la jungla como blancos para atacar y atravesarlos con tu cuerno. Los problemas son el método de la jungla para darte una gran satisfacción, conforme los vas superando y destruyendo. Esta es tu oportunidad para ser un poco agresivo. No sólo resuelve tus problemas, ¡DEMUÉLELOS!
¿Puedes imaginar una jungla donde todo sea fácil? ¡No seríamos rinos, seríamos hipopótamos! *Hay* una jungla allá afuera y es desafiante. Cada día late con energía y emoción y eso es lo que los rinos necesitamos para enriquecernos. Las vacas pueden sentarse a pastar y tratar de vivir una existencia sin riesgos, pero a la larga descubrirán la insensatez de cambiar su libertad por su vida.
La jungla es salvaje, es verdad. La jungla puede ser fea y peligrosa, cierto; pero, al mismo tiempo, puede ser inspiradoramente majestuosa y muy gratificante. Más que nada y sobre todo, la jungla es libre.

Capítulo 3

CONOCE A TU GUÍA PARA EL SAFARI

Ningún safari a través de la selva estaría completo sin un guía bien informado y experimentado, y yo tengo justo lo que estás buscando. La mayoría de ustedes ya considera a Jesús como su guía de expedición, así que ya están listos, pero para aquellos que no han tenido el tiempo de buscar a un buen guía del safari o simplemente olvidaron que necesitan un guía, les tengo buenas noticias: a través de Jesucristo, Dios todavía puede acomodarte en su agenda.

Dios es la protección total de los peligros de la jungla, y Él tiene un profundo sentido del conocimiento y del entendimiento. Todos los rinos exitosos tienen a Dios como su guía en el safari. ¡No te conformes con menos! Hay ciertas cosas que no te puedes dar el lujo de economizar y ésta es una de ellas. Puedes prescindir de tu cantimplora, pero no olvides hacer arreglos para que Dios te guíe. Puedes pasar por alto las indicaciones de tu mapa, pero asegúrate de que Dios esté siempre contigo.

NADIE LO HACE MEJOR

Nunca aceptes guías inferiores e irresponsables o tu safari entero terminará en tragedia. Hay muchos peligros inesperados a los que te enfrentarás. Viajar en la jungla sin la guía de Dios te traerá confusión, penurias, frustración y a la larga, la muerte. ¿Por qué exponerte a todo eso, cuando Dios está tan disponible, tan dispuesto y tan fácil de contactar para ser tu guía en el safari? Además, ¡Él es un tipo agradable!

Recuerda que Dios creó la jungla. Nadie la conoce mejor que Él. Es su trabajo de tiempo completo el guiar a los animales a través de la jungla y se sentiría lastimado si no acudes a Él para que te ayude. ¡Él es muy adaptable, no come mucho, tiene muchas influencias, está disponible las 24 horas del día, y es capaz de hacer milagros!

NO ENVÍES DINERO

Para contactar a Dios como guía de tu safari, no tienes que telefonearlo (Dios es el operador del primer teléfono inalámbrico), no tienes que enviarle una carta (en ocasiones no puedes esperar tanto tiempo) y tampoco tienes que ir a su oficina. Dios viaja extensamente, así que para reducir sus gastos, no tiene oficina.

Todo lo que tienes que hacer es saber que Dios envió a su hijo Jesucristo a la tierra para salvarnos, y pedirle a Jesús que entre a tu corazón como tu Señor y Salvador particular y que tome control de tu vida. Ahí está la vieja ley de la oferta y la demanda. Él va donde es requerido. Inclúyelo en todos tus planes y Él estará contigo puntualmente. Si tú te preguntas cómo hace Él todo, sólo recuerda que "con Dios todo es posible". El manejo efectivo del tiempo también funciona, supongo, pero cualquiera que sea Su método, no hay sentimiento más tranquilizador que saber que Dios está cuidando de ti. ¡El Rinoceronte más grandioso del mundo está de tu lado! Él es tu confidente, tu socio, tu consejero, tu compañero, tu amigo, y Él te ama.

LEE SU LIBRO

Dios es un verdadero personaje también. Para poder entender mejor de dónde viene Él, debes leer un libro que Él ha difundido como "La Biblia." Sé que le ha ido muy bien con él. Ha encontrado muy buenos impresores, ha establecido fantásticos canales de distribución, ha encontrado el respaldo financiero, ¡y este libro ha sido un éxito de ventas consistente durante miles de años! Es difícil prosperar en el campo editorial en esta época, así que es obvio que Él conoce todos los trucos. Lee la Biblia y pon especial atención a la historia de Jesucristo porque si conoces a Jesús, conocerás a Dios. Tú estarás orgulloso de que Él sea tu guía para el safari.

"Dios es tu socio, tu consejero, tu amigo, tu compañero, y Él te ama"

Capítulo 4

LA CACERÍA

Aún antes de empezar tu expedición a través de la jungla, debes saber lo que estás buscando. Esto tiene sentido ¿cierto? Si vas por ahí vagando, perdido en la jungla, estás expuesto a ser la presa del cazador. No permitas que eso te suceda. ¡Debes saber lo que quieres cazar! Si no sabes lo que buscas ¿cómo saber qué tipo de municiones llevar? ¿Cómo saber dónde empezar a buscar si ni siquiera sabes qué estás buscando? ¿Cómo sabrás si lo atrapas? Si no sabes lo que estás cazando, ¿qué diablos estás haciendo en la jungla?

SIGUE ATACANDO O SERÁS DEVORADO VIVO

Debes conocer lo que persigues, de otra manera la jungla te devorará. ¡Si no te mueves, la tierra movediza te tragará por completo, con todo y tu gruesa piel! Manténte activo. Que tus cuatro patas sigan gozando de la tierra de la jungla, abriendo una senda a través del grueso follaje.

Conoce lo que buscas y sigue tras esto implacable, incansable y decidido o se te escabullirá entre la maleza y te expondrás a perderlo para siempre. Puedes perderlo de vista por un momento, pero NUNCA, NUNCA, NUNCA dejes de atacarlo.

Puede que ya no lo oigas o lo huelas, pero sigue atacando de todas maneras. ¡Ahí está! Está escondido observando cómo te vas acercando, listo para escapar cuando te acerques demasiado. Pero si te detienes ahora, si no sigues en este punto, cuando estás tan cerca de atraparlo, él se reirá en tu cara y se burlará de ti.

PURA MOTIVACIÓN

Conoce lo que persigues y nunca dejes de acosarlo hasta que sea tuyo, nunca dejes la cacería hasta que lo tengas trinchado en tu cuerno como a un murciélago en un palito. Que la energía siga fluyendo. No permitas que la enfermedad de las vacas, la inercia, te agobie hasta hacerte desistir o la jungla te consumirá.

La jungla se caracteriza por su energía y movimiento. Se alimenta de la vida y, si tú aflojas el paso, la jungla no tendrá piedad de tu inservible cuerpo, de tus cansados huesos... Los buitres, al percibir la debilidad, descenderán sobre tu cuerpo y te acabarán. Mantén tus 2,500 kilos moviéndose a buen paso para que cualquier ser viviente sepa que tú eres una parte vital y funcionando en la jungla.

En conclusión, debes saber lo que persigues y continuar acosándolo o las fuerzas de la naturaleza harán de tu cacería un desastre. Sigue moviéndote hacia adelante, nunca te detengas o el sol de la jungla cocerá tu cuerpo consumiendo hasta el último pedacito de energía que te quede. Sigue atacando y la brisa que provoques te mantendrá cómodo y fresco. Por otro lado, baja la velocidad y los insectos se pararan sobre tus ojos, el sol quemará tu piel, las aves de rapiña te observarán vorazmente y la jungla hará su trabajo para mantener a los desertores fuera de sus fronteras.

Esto suena brutal, ¿cierto? Yo no pretendo convertirte en un manojo de nervios o hacerte difícil conciliar el sueño en la noche por miedo a que un buitre mordisquee tu cuerpo o un zancudo se pare sobre tu ojo, pero debo hacer que sigas atacando. Este es un libro motivacional. Estoy tratando de que valga la pena lo que pagaste por él.

TE ESTÁS DIVIRTIENDO

Por supuesto la parte más divertida de la cacería en un safari es la persecución. Una vez que hayas atrapado lo que buscabas, se acaba toda la emoción. Es como escalar la montaña más alta: escalar es muy divertido, pero ¿qué haces cuando llegas a la cima? Puedes disfrutar la vista, pero eso se acaba muy rápido.

Recuerdo cuando era niño haber ido en auto con mi familia hasta el Gran Cañón. Fue divertido... hasta que llegamos allá. El Gran Cañón es tan viejo como se ve desde lejos.

"Tú eres exitoso si te encuentras en la jungla persiguiendo tus objetivos"

Si recuerdas algunos de tus más grandes logros, te acordarás del camino que recorriste para obtenerlos como la parte emocionante del proceso. Son los cuentos que te llevan hasta la presa los que hacen al safari tan emocionante. Ir a un safari en donde la presa está atada a un árbol esperando a que llegues y le dispares no sería muy divertido ¿cierto?

El refrán que dice que "el éxito es un viaje, no un destino", es totalmente cierto. Eres exitoso si te encuentras en la jungla persiguiendo tus objetivos. ¡Desafortunadamente puede que ahora no te des cuenta, pero te la estás pasando de maravilla!

Capítulo 5

RENUNCIA A TU EMPLEO

Hace un momento veía un programa en la televisión donde preguntaban a los niños si sabían la diferencia entre trabajar y jugar. ¿Tú conoces la diferencia? Un chico, evidentemente muy brillante, contestó que "el trabajo es hacer cosas que otros me ordenan, y jugar es hacer cosas que yo quiero hacer." ¿Acaso no es esta una gran respuesta?

Claro que sería poco realista de mi parte sugerir que todo el mundo se la pase haciendo "lo que se le antoje." Algunos tendrán que pasarse la vida llevando a cabo las tareas desagradables y viviendo una vida de monotonía, ¿cierto?

Estas son las vacas. Las vacas son tan naturales como la muerte y la enfermedad. ¡No podríamos valorar a animales emocionantes y vivos como los rinos si no tuviéramos a animales como las vacas para comprarlos! A pesar de su falta de atractivo y sus formas poco atrayentes, en realidad necesitamos a las vacas.

LAS VACAS NECESITAN SEGURIDAD

Las vacas son las únicas dispuestas a cambiar su libertad por un sueldo seguro. Ellas son felices trabajando para otros porque necesitan que las dirijan, necesitan ser guiadas, y sobreviven dejando que otros las cuiden. Dale a una vaca un sueldo regular, unos días de vacaciones pagadas al año, seguro médico, y tal vez un pequeño seguro de vida ¡y esa vaca te dará la vida!

¿Lo ves?, las vacas son buenas para algo porque ¿quién más trabajaría para ti? ¡A las vacas les han lavado el cerebro para que crean que deben trabajar para vivir! Ellas no saben que tienen otras opciones. Cuando tú haces lo que te gusta, no es trabajo. ¿Por qué entonces pasarte la vida haciendo algo desagradable?

EL EMPRESARIO CONTRA LA SUPERVACA

En la jungla, tú puedes ser el que haga lo que otros le dicen que haga, o bien el que les diga a los otros lo que tienen que hacer. Esto último es el trabajo del empresario. Ser empresario es el punto más gratificante, divertido y emocionante en la jungla.

Pero ¿a cuántos niños has oído decir que quieren ser empresarios cuando sean grandes? Muy muy pocos, estoy seguro. Yo ni siquiera había escuchado la palabra "empresario" hasta que salí de la preparatoria porque las escuelas públicas son establecidas y dirigidas por el gobierno que es la tierra de pastura para vacas más grande en las Junglas Unidas de América. De hecho, las vacas que trabajan para el gobierno no son vacas ordinarias. ¡Son supervacas!

Por lo menos las vacas que trabajan en la iniciativa privada ayudan a crear un producto o servicio que beneficia a todos los animales en la jungla. Estas vacas trabajan con cierta competencia, Y REALMENTE TRABAJAN, porque si no lo hacen, las despiden de su pastura. Ese no es el caso de la supervacas del gobierno.

NO TODOS LOS ANIMALES FUERON CREADOS IGUALES

Las supervacas son una raza extremadamente fea y repugnante de vaca, porque ellas no producen absolutamente nada y sí roban a la población de la jungla para pagar sus imperios burocráticos que regulan e interfieren en las vidas de todos los animales. ¿Te das cuenta porque no sería en el mejor interés de este despreciable animal enseñarles a los pequeños animales acerca de las oportunidades de nuestro sistema de libre empresa y alentar al joven empresario?

Los rinocerontes empresarios se preocupan por las supervacas. Después de todo, el único propósito en la vida de la supervaca es obstruir y limitar, para "proteger" y para gobernar, e intentar crear igualdad en una jungla desigual. La igualdad de derechos es lo que nosotros queremos, y no tratar de hacer a todos los animales iguales. Todo lo que la

"La supervaca burocrática es la peor vaca que existe"

vaca representa va en contra de la fibra moral del empresario. Desgraciadamente, las vacas comunes y corrientes alientan la proliferación y actividad de las supervacas ya que, naturalmente, el sueño de la mayoría de las vacas es ser supervacas. Ser una supervaca significa mayor seguridad, más pago, beneficios adicionales y menos trabajo.

Pero conforme más y más rinos se van hartando de las supervacas parasitarias, la existencia de la supervaca está en peligro. De hecho, estamos viviendo los comienzos de la Revolución Rinoceróntica, en la cual las supervacas serán reducidas a simples vacas. En un capítulo posterior hablaremos de eso.

¿TE GUSTA TU TRABAJO?

Si este capítulo te ha molestado, por favor tenme paciencia porque siempre hay excepciones. Primero que nada, déjame aclarar mis puntos de vista con respecto al trabajo. Sólo porque alguien tenga un empleo trabajando para alguien más, no lo califica automáticamente como una vaca. Algunos animales de verdad disfrutan su trabajo. Algunos lo encuentran fascinante y no podrían estar más felices. Algunos tal vez hasta pagarían por el privilegio de hacer lo que hacen. ¡Oye, si esa es la posición en que tú te encuentras, eso es grandioso! ¡Sigue cargando!

Pero si te pasas cinco días a la semana haciendo algo aburrido, que no disfrutas, que te hace sentirte miserable, entonces lo siento, ¡pero tú eres una vaca! ¡Un verdadero rino no desperdiciaría su vida de esa manera! ¡Nadie te está torciendo la mano! ¡No estás atado a un árbol! ¡No necesitas permiso para ir al baño! ¡Tú tienes el poder para elegir y estás viviendo en una jungla donde todavía tienes la libertad de hacer esa elección! Si no disfrutas lo que haces a diario ¿POR QUÉ lo haces? Porque eres una vaca, ¡esa es la razón! ¡Eres una llorona, cobarde y vacuna vaca de piel delgada!

No dejes que yo lastime tus sentimientos, pero sí trata de molestarte porque tal vez si te enojas lo suficiente, la vergüenza o la rabia haga que tu sangre empiece a correr, tal vez si te disgustas lo suficiente de ser una vaca, tomarás acción. ¡Tal vez hasta renuncies! ¡Anda, hazlo!

UNA PARED POR CADA MONTACARGAS POR FAVOR

Recuerdo uno de mis primeros empleos de los que renuncié. Justo después de terminar la preparatoria, trabajé en una compañía de computadoras en el departamento de admisión. Mi trabajo consistía en descargar los camiones y procesar todo el material que ingresaba. Yo manejaba el montacargas, lo cual era divertido. Mientras aprendía a operarlo, atravesé una pared, lo cual fue emocionante. Se permite atravesar la pared con un montacargas solamente una vez, así que la emoción de manejarlo se terminó pronto.

"Se permite atravesar la pared con un montacargas solamente una vez, así que la emoción de manejarlo se terminó pronto"

Siendo un rinoceronte en desarrollo, busqué nuevos territorios para cargar y así fue como me ascendieron al almacén después de seis meses en el departamento de admisión. Dos meses después de eso, fui ascendido a despachador. Ahora bien, si alguna vez existió un puesto creado especialmente para generar colapsos nerviosos, ese era el empleo de despachador. La función del despachador es, lógicamente, despachar.

Yo estaba a cargo de ver que la producción fluyera suavemente desde el departamento de admisión hasta el almacén, luego a la planta de montaje, al departamento de pruebas, de regreso al departamento de reelaboración y, finalmente, si todo estaba bien, a envíos. Lo primero que aprendí es que la producción NUNCA fluye suavemente. Uno de mis mayores retos mientras corría entre los diferentes departamentos de manufactura era averiguar el origen de lo que llamábamos "Déficitis". Sólo había una cosa de la que nunca estábamos escasos, y esto era precisamente los déficits.

Naturalmente, todos en la compañía odian al despachador. Yo tenía que estar constantemente fastidiando, suplicando, consiguiendo y exigiendo el trabajo para que saliera a tiempo de la planta de producción, y así cumplir con las fechas límite. Cuando las computadoras no estaban a tiempo, ya sabes de quién era la culpa.

Un día reventé. En esa época yo compartía una oficina con otro despachador de piel gruesa, la cual era mucho más gruesa que la mía en aquel entonces. Nuestros escritorios estaban llenos, hasta el tope, con pedidos "urgentes" y reportes de piezas agotadas, los teléfonos sonaban todo el tiempo para reportar solamente problemas, ambos trabajábamos entre 10 y 12 horas al día, y de pronto todas estas dificultades me vencieron. Solamente puse mi cabeza sobre el escritorio y empecé a sollozar sin control, tan fuerte como el timbre del teléfono. No recuerdo lo que mi compañero me dijo para calmarme. Tal vez fue algo como, "¡No seas tan vaca, Scott!"

MI PRIMER NEGOCIO

Me recuperé de esto para continuar el trabajo y fue entonces cuando conocí a Kim. Después de salir con ella algunos meses, me enteré de que Kim peluqueaba perros. Siendo un empresario prometedor, aproveché la situación y le pedí a Kim que fuera mi novia. ¡Esto era grandioso! ¡Ahora tenía una novia que podía peluquear poodles!

Mi siguiente paso fue sugerir que pusiéramos nuestro propio negocio –¡tal vez una estética para perros! ¡Sensacional! ¡Ésta era mi oportunidad de renunciar a mi empleo de despachador y poner a Kim a trabajar! Le dije que la llamaríamos "Estética de Kim" y eso cerró el trato.

El lunes fui a trabajar y les avisé que renunciaba en dos semanas. ¡Qué sentimiento tan estimulante! Mi supervisor se sentó conmigo y me habló del fantástico futuro que tendría si me quedaba en la compañía. Él dijo que muy pronto me ascenderían a diseñador de producción. Cuando él oyó mis planes de poner una estética para perros, realmente trató de convencerme de que me quedara, pero yo fui inflexible y en dos semanas obtendría mi libertad.

Y así fue como nació la "Estética de Kim". Éste fue mi primer descubrimiento en la ciencia de la motivación, porque yo tenía que hacer algo ¿cierto? ¡Y yo no sabía peluquear perros! Además, pronto descubrí que la cantidad de perros que Kim peluqueaba estaba relacionada directamente con la cantidad de dinero que ganaría. Sin embargo, sólo contábamos con seis dólares por cada perro y Kim era tan perfeccionista que sólo podía terminar tres perros al día, sin importar cuánto intentara motivarla.

MI PRIMER NEGOCIO FRACASA

Después de seis meses nuestro negocio se había ido a la ruina. No tenía dinero, Kim no tenía ganas de peluquear más poodles y me encontré de regreso en la compañía de computadoras pidiéndole a mi supervisor que me regresara a mi empleo. Le dije que reconocía mi error, que en verdad yo estaría en mejores condiciones con ellos, y que nunca querría ver otro poodle en toda mi vida. ¡Y era cierto... la parte de no querer volver a ver un poodle nunca más!

La semana siguiente fui el Señor Despachador otra vez, sólo que esta vez fue peor, ya que ahora ya había vivido la verdadera libertad y el placer de ser mi propio jefe. Mi adicción por ser empresario ya había echado raíces ¡Yo había saboreado el filete mientras los demás estaban rumiando hamburguesas! ¡Yo había sentido el cielo, y los demás sólo conocían el infierno! ¡TENÍA que salir otra vez!

EMPIEZO A SABOREAR EL FILETE OTRA VEZ

Entonces otra idea vino a mi: Poner un autolavado móvil. ¡Eso es lo que haría! Instalaría tanques de agua, bombas y mangueras en la parte de atrás de mi camión y lavaría los autos de los ejecutivos en los estacionamientos de sus oficinas. Les conté a algunos amigos del trabajo acerca de mis planes y ellos me dijeron que era una idea tonta.

"¿Cómo vas a lavar coches bajo el sol sin que se marquen las manchas de agua?" preguntaban. "¡Nadie te pagará cinco dólares por lavarle el coche! ¡No puedes obtener jabón en el estacionamiento! ¡No puedes hacerlo porque salpicas a otros coches! ¡Hay escasez de agua y la delegación no te permitirá hacerlo! ¡Nunca funcionará!

Dejé de hablarles a mis amigos acerca de esto y el lunes en la mañana fui a decirle a mi supervisor que me iba otra vez. Ésta vez no me dijo qué maravilloso futuro me esperaba ahí. Más bien disgustado, me dijo que no podría regresar y obtener un empleo en esa compañía. ¡Este era el fin! Me pareció perfecto y en dos semanas yo era libre otra vez.

EN BUSCA DE CAPITAL

Ahora tenía que pedir prestado algo de dinero. Fui al banco donde había terminado de pagar el préstamo para mi camión. Ellos me habían enviado una carta insistiendo en que siempre les pidiera dinero prestado a ellos, ¡sin falta!

No esperé tener problemas para obtener los fondos que requería.

Confiadamente entré al banco y le conté al encargado de préstamos todo acerca de mis planes para poner un autolavado móvil, y le pregunté acerca de un préstamo para echarlo a andar. El banquero se puso tenso, se recargó en el respaldo de su silla y me preguntó si podría darle una declaración.

Le dije, "¡Por supuesto... me siento muy optimista!"

Aparentemente esa no era la clase de declaración que él quería porque no obtuve el préstamo. Después de que otros tres bancos me rechazaron, empecé a ponerme nervioso. Te lo digo, si alguna vez tienen que hacerte un trasplante de corazón, pide un corazón de banquero porque no están muy gastados.

"Tal vez yo debería de haber pensado en este detalle antes de renunciar a mi empleo," empecé a pensar. En ese tiempo yo tenía 20 años y todavía vivía con mis padres. No les dije que había dejado mi empleo por miedo a que me desheredaran. Así que cada mañana me levantaba como de costumbre y salía de mi casa como si me fuera a trabajar.

Pasó una semana y era claro que ningún banco me prestaría el dinero. Sintiéndome desesperado, fui a casa de mis abuelos y les conté toda la historia. Obtuve el dinero... quinientos dólares.

ME CASÉ CON UNA RINO

Los siguientes tres años fueron muy emocionantes. Kim y yo nos casamos y nos fuimos a Australia de luna de miel por un mes. Regresamos y empezamos a administrar el autolavado móvil juntos. Sólo que esta vez, a Kim le tocaba la parte motivadora y yo hacía el trabajo.

En un año, teníamos dos camiones y dos rutas llenas. Contraté a mi hermano menor, Gregg, para que me ayudara, y juntos empezamos a ganar mucho dinero. Con el tiempo empezamos a cobrar quince dólares por lavada y teníamos a todos los clientes en un programa semanal. El negocio iba mejor y entonces contratamos al hermano menor de Kim, Larry, para empezar otra ruta. Para este momento ya habíamos salido en los periódicos, y la revista nacional había escrito un pequeño artículo sobre nosotros. Después me entrevistaron en la televisión y nuestro negocio hasta fue mencionado en un par de libros. Estábamos en la cima... ¡y ellos dijeron que nunca funcionaría!

Ahora, al mirar atrás, me dan escalofríos al pensar que si no hubiera tenido la audacia de renunciar a mi empleo, ¡tal vez todavía sería un despachador! *Si tú odias tu trabajo,* busca otro, o pon tu propio negocio. ¡Sólo atrévete!

NO CONTRIBUYAS A LA BUROCRACIA

Para terminar, me doy cuenta de que indudablemente hay muchas excepciones a la regla de que cualquiera que trabaje para el gobierno es una supervaca. Probablemente las excepciones más grandes serían aquéllos que sirven en los servicios militares (El Ejército, La Marina, La Fuerza Aérea, etc.) El gobierno sí juega un papel importante en esto. Es la burocracia que crea los reglamentos y trámites lo que no necesitamos. Si trabajas para la burocracia, lo mejor que podrías hacer por las Junglas Unidas de América sería que renunciaras a tu empleo y obtuvieras uno en la iniciativa privada, o que pusieras tu propio negocio. De esta forma, estarías ayudando a crear productos y servicios que nosotros, los animales, queremos o necesitamos, y no servicios que nos imponen.

Capítulo 6

EL MIEDO A SER APLASTADO

Ser un rino significa estar automotivado. Ahora bien, hay una gran diferencia entre automotivación y sólo simple motivación. Antes que nada, ¿qué es exactamente motivación? Bueno, el diccionario dice que "motivación" es *"la condición de estar motivado."* Esa es una típica definición de diccionario: no te dice nada. Bien, vamos a jugar su juego entonces. ¿Qué significa "estar motivado"? El diccionario dice que: "motivar" significa *"proporcionar un motivo."* Ya nos estamos acercando. Entonces, querido diccionario, ¿qué es un "motivo"? Aquí viene la parte sustancial. Esto es a lo que se reduce el ser exitoso. Un motivo es *"algo que hace que una persona actúe"* Por supuesto, al decir "persona" quieren decir "rinoceronte". Este es sin duda un error tipográfico que seguramente será corregido en la próxima edición.

Por lo tanto, motivación es proporcionarte a ti mismo algo que hará que actúes. La siguiente historia ilustra cómo la mayoría de los seres son motivados.

LA HISTORIA DE LA RANITA VERDE

Al parecer, una ranita verde había caído en un surco que se encontraba en una carretera y no podía brincar lo suficientemente alto para salir. Sus amigas ranas estaban arriba de la zona animándola a salir.

"¡Vamos! ¡Tú puedes!" le gritaban al unísono y a todo pulmón. La ranita brincaba tan alto como podía, pero simplemente no era suficiente, a pesar del estímulo y consejo de todas las ranas. Dos horas después, la rana seguía en la zanja y sus amigas ya no podían esperar más. Se alejaron brincando, dejándola ahí.

Más tarde, justo cuando se preparaban a andar en el lago y a croar un rato, las ranas vieron a su pequeña amiga que había quedado atrapada en la zanja. Suponiendo que ella nunca habría podido salir de ahí, exclamaron emocionadas, "¿Qué pasó? ¿cómo saliste de la zanja?" la rana volteó y les dijo, "¡Un gran camión venía por la carretera y yo tuve que salir!"

NO DEJES QUE TE APLASTEN

¡Fue el miedo de ser aplastada lo que hizo que la rana actuara! Si lo piensas un momento, ¿no es así como la mayoría, especialmente las vacas, se motivan? ¡Es el miedo a ser aplastado! En la escuela, los niños hacen su tarea y estudian para no reprobar. En este caso, un "5" significa ser aplastado.

Cuando estos niños salgan de la escuela, buscarán un empleo para ganar dinero. La motivación en esta caso es el miedo a morirse de hambre, y trabajan sólo lo suficiente para no ser despedidos, lo cual sería otra forma de ser aplastados. Si analizas porqué la mayoría de los animales hacen algo, por lo general se resume en el miedo a ser aplastado.

Ahora bien, no estoy diciendo que eso sea indeseable. Muchas veces eso es lo que se necesita para salir de una zanja. Un hombre de negocios que teme ante la perspectiva de la bancarrota estará motivado. ¿Cierto? Si él no empieza a hacer algo, entonces se verá directamente involucrado en una gran caída, ¡la propia!

Mi punto es: ¿qué es lo que va a motivar a la rana ahora que está fuera de zanja y que el peligro de ser aplastada ya no existe? Ahora la rana está en el lago disfrutando y tomando las cosas con calma. ¿Recuerdas la enfermedad de las vacas, la inercia? La tendencia de todos los objetos, incluyéndonos a nosotros, es quedarse quietos. Este es un hecho científico. Una vez que el peligro de ser aplastados, el cual hizo que actuáramos, se ha ido, nuestra tendencia es dejar de actuar y no hacer nada.

SÉ ARROLLADOR, NO SEAS ARROLLADO

Es aquí donde los rinos se separan de las vacas, porque los rinos están AUTOMOTIVADOS. ¡Ellos SIGUEN AVANZANDO! ¿por qué esperar a que nos aplasten otra vez? Esa es una forma terrible de ir por la vida. Este tipo de motivación puede darte muchas noches de insomnio. Es mejor estar automotivado y exceder por mucho ese punto donde el miedo a ser aplastado es tu impulso para actuar.

Por lo tanto, necesitas proporcionarte a ti mismo un incentivo para seguir cargando. Los rinocerontes no sólo hacen lo estrictamente necesario para irla pasando, como lo hacen las vacas. Cualquier cosa que hagan los rinos, la hacen a fondo, a todo vapor, ¡y les importa muy poco que vengan los torpedos!

¿Qué es lo que te impulsará a ti a cargar de esa manera? ¿Tienes una razón lo suficientemente buena? ¡Tú *sabes* que si no actúas, no hay ABSOLUTAMENTE NINGUNA ESPERANZA para ti! ¡No seas como el caballo que pudo conectar un hit, pero no corrió! ¡*Tienes* que actuar! No tienes alternativa. Está ahí en el diccionario. Búscalo por ti mismo si no me crees.

¿HAY UN DOCTOR EN CASA?

Indudablemente, habrá momentos cuando tus motores empiecen a bajar la velocidad. Perderás interés en tus proyectos y tu energía descenderá a un nivel peligroso. Sentarse en la casa a ver televisión y comer pan danés puede sonarte muy atractivo y hasta puede que te permitas a ti mismo ocuparte en tal decadencia.

¡Cuidado! La enfermedad de las vacas, la inercia, ha entrado en tu torrente sanguíneo, ya sea debido a que te asociaste con vacas, o bien puede ser que lo hayas contraído en el asiento de un excusado sucio en alguna gasolinera por ahí. Ahora estás en una etapa crítica. La inercia es capaz de invadir todo tu sistema y reducirte a un estado bovino a menos que puedas luchar contra ella con todo tu espíritu de rinoceronte indomable.

Si te encuentras con un fuerte caso de inercia, donde es casi demasiado esfuerzo leer este libro, menos aún hacer cualquier otra cosa, y no hay un Doctor en Rinocerología presente, escúchame. ¿En realidad quieres ser una vaca? ¿Acaso disfrutas quedándote vencido y echado sobre tu propio estiércol? ¿Tu idea de diversión es atrofiarte y pudrirte como un montón de repugnantes desechos? Las vacas son lo más bajo en lo que puedes caer. ¡Son más bajas que los desechos de ballenas! ¿Quieres caer tan bajo?

¿O quieres ser un rinoceronte desbordando energía, viviendo una vida feliz, útil, emocionante y productiva? ¿Quieres que la sangre corra por tu cuerpo otra vez enriqueciendo todas tus células para volverlas a la vida? ¿Quieres vivir e intentarlo, o quieres darte por vencido y morir?

INVIERTE ALGO DE ENERGÍA EN TI MISMO

Si la idea de ser una vaca verdaderamente te repugna, ACTÚA AHORA o la inercia te hará caer de nuevo. Si no tienes nada más que hacer, ponte tus shorts y tus tenis y vete a correr. ¡Sólo empieza a correr! Gastar energía crea más energía. Tienes que descargar tu fuerza, tienes que reunir más vigor. La flojera y la energía son opuestas. Como el agua y el aceite, no se mezclan. Como el agua y el fuego, pueden destruirse mutuamente. ¡Quema tu aceite!

¡Estuvo cerca! ¿Cierto? ¡Por poco te perdemos! ¿Cómo te sientes ahora? Tu cuerno estaba empezando a caerse, estabas perdiendo rápidamente, y tu piel se empezaba a ver más delgada en algunas partes. Lo mejor para ti ahora es muchos líquidos y NADA DE DESCANSO. ¡CUANDO YA HAYAS CALENTADO, NO TE DETENGAS! Mantén el fuego incontenible y el aceite ardiendo. ¡Sigue cargando!

QUÍMICA MOTIVACIONAL

La mejor manera de mantener tu fuego encendido y tu máquina zumbando es usar las mismas emociones que te permitieron no ser aplastado. La ira, el miedo y la vergüenza son emociones muy poderosas que te harán seguir adelante. Piensa por un momento en los cambios que tu cuerpo sufre cuando te enojas. Tu cerebro envía una hormona llamada noradrenalina a través de todo tu cuerpo la cual hace que tu corazón empiece a latir más rápido. Empiezas a respirar con más velocidad. Tus pupilas se dilatan y tu digestión se detiene. ¡Ahora estás listo para la acción! Cuando estás en estas condiciones, no te acuestas a dormir. Te sientes con ganas de destruir una pared. Sin embargo, en vez de hacer eso, utiliza esa repentina ola de fuerza para tu provecho, para ayudarte a impulsarte hacia adelante.

TU MEJOR REVANCHA

Cuando empezaba a construir mi negocio de autolavado móvil mis motores impulsores fueron, entre otros, las vacas que me dijeron que jamás funcionaría. Sus burlas fueron mi motivación. Creo que fue Frank Sinatra el que dijo: "La mejor venganza es el éxito consistente."

Para poder aprovechar este tipo de motivación, guarda una "lista de afrentas". Tú vas a tener éxito, tú vas a triunfar, tú vas a prevalecer A PESAR de estas vacas. Haz una lista detallada de todos los que dudan de lo que dices que vas a realizar, una lista de todos los que se ríen de tus planes, de los que cuestionan tus habilidades, y después haz lo que dijiste que harías y déjalos atrás asfixiándose con tu polvo. Adelántate tanto a ellos que se queden en un estado de estupefacción y luego olvídalos. Sólo son vacas.

Debo sonar como un verdadero malvado. En realidad soy un tipo adorable. Es sólo que, como Steve Martin dice, "La motivación no es bonita."

"Si no tienes nada más que hacer, ponte tu equipo para correr y vete a correr"

Capítulo 7

EL JUEGO DE LA LIBRE EMPRESA

La vida en la jungla puede ser un juego o una batalla. Es tu elección. ¿En cuál de los dos prefieres participar? Yo personalmente prefiero involucrarme en un juego que en una sangrienta batalla. De hecho, es sólo la manera de ver las cosas. Todos nosotros, seamos vacas o magníficos rinocerontes, tenemos que jugar el juego bajo las mismas reglas. Aquí en las Junglas Unidas de América, jugamos el juego de la libre empresa, el cual opera en el mundo capitalista usando dinero.

Por supuesto, el dinero es sólo un "medio de intercambio". Por sí sólo, el dinero no tiene ningún valor. Son los bienes y servicios que éste representa los que le dan valor. Podríamos haber usado pollos en lugar de dólares, pero habría sido poco práctico en ciertas situaciones. Para poder funcionar con este medio de intercambio debes saber la regla básica del juego de la libre empresa que es simplemente: *debes dar para obtener*. En realidad no existe eso del almuerzo gratis, contrariamente a lo que el gobierno pretende que tú creas.

"Podríamos haber utilizado pollos en lugar de dólares, pero habría sido poco práctico en ciertas situaciones."

Es este simple sistema de iniciativa privada lo que ha construido nuestra gran jungla. Los americanos disfrutamos una libertad que no se encuentra en ningún otro lugar del mundo. Sin embargo, hay supervacas allá afuera a quienes les gustaría reducirnos a un estado de beneficencia bovina y lo harían si pudieran. Es nuestro deber como rinocerontes ver que estas vacas se queden en su lugar. Se lo debemos a nuestros rinos fundadores y a los futuros rinos de América el asegurarnos de que el gobierno sea restringido porque de otro modo éste crecerá y se hará más costoso, y seguirá interfiriendo en los asuntos privados y de negocios de todos nosotros.

EL GOBIERNO ES TU ENEMIGO

El único enemigo del rinoceronte es un gobierno todo poderoso y envanecido que amenaza a nuestra libertad. Nuestra mejor estrategia es ignorar el gobierno. Procura tener que ver con él lo menos posible. Son las vacas, quienes constantemente buscan al gobierno para que les resuelva sus problemas, las alimenten y las vistan, y que piden ayuda para todos sus intereses particulares, las que animan al gobierno a hacer cosas que nuestros rinos fundadores nunca pretendieron hacer. De esta forma, el gobierno sofoca a la libertad. Los rinos necesitan de la libertad de la jungla para cargar. NUNCA permitamos que nos acorralen junto con las vacas dentro de esa falsa seguridad de una pastura llena de abono.

PREPÁRATE PARA SER EXPLOTADO

En ocasiones sabrás de alguna supervaca profesional que te dirá que los ricos acumulan su riqueza explotando a los pobres. ¿No es esa la afirmación más estúpida que hayas oído? Si entiendes la regla del juego de la libre empresa –DEBES DAR PARA RECIBIR–, podrás darte cuenta de que son aquéllos quienes deciden no participar en el juego (los pobres que se quejan), quienes explotan a aquéllos que si participamos (los ricos productores). ¡Los pobres no tienen nada para ser explotados! Somos los contribuyentes, los ricos, quienes pagamos impuestos, los que damos a los pobres los cheques de beneficencia. ¡Eso es explotación!

Los pobres siguen explotando a los ricos que arriesgan su dinero y su energía para poner negocios y generar empleos. Los productores construyen hospitales, centros comerciales, bibliotecas, parque y todo lo que hace la vida más agradable. Y todo esto es para disfrute de los pobres.

HAZ TU PROPIA EXPLOTACIÓN

Conoce la jungla. Entre más conozcas tu mundo y entiendas cómo funciona, mejor preparado estarás para explotarlo. Debes saber dónde se encuentran los abrevaderos para que no mueras de sed. Debes conocer las parte más densas de la jungla donde puedas encontrar un lugar para descansar. Hasta los rinos necesitan darse un respiro de vez en cuando. Debes saber qué animales viven en qué parte de la jungla y cuáles son los amigos de los rinocerontes. Debes saber dónde se encuentran las partes más bonitas y frondosas de la jungla para que construyas tu casa ahí. Los rinos no viven en el estéril y árido desierto. (A menos que haya un abrevadero privado ahí, por supuesto). Asegúrate de que estás donde debes.

Conoce la jungla para que puedas sacar provecho de ella. Tu jungla de concreto consiste de vías rápidas, miles de negocios que te ofrecen una innumerable cantidad de productos y servicios, millones de animales con dinero para comprar, y millones de animales que quieren trabajar. La tarea del rino empresario es dar a los animales desempleados un trabajo que hacer y a los animales cargados de dinero algo que comprar.

Los animales con educación universitaria dependen en gran medida de los rinocerontes que gustan de la actividad empresarial. Alguien tiene que construir los negocios y las corporaciones donde los abogados y ejecutivos puedan trabajar. Alguien tiene que construir esta jungla, y crear así algo bueno para todos, para que las supervacas intelectuales y liberales tengan algo que criticar y de qué quejarse. Si nosotros no lo construimos, ¿quién lo hará?

TÚ NACISTE CON UN CUERNO

Sabemos lo que significa ser un rinoceronte. Los rinos son los productores, los promotores y los constructores, los responsables del progreso del mundo. Tenemos una gran responsabilidad, ¿cierto? Si no fuera por nosotros los rinos, el mundo estaría en un estado deplorable, ¿no crees? Imagínate si las vacas tuvieran las riendas del mundo. ¡Estaríamos hasta el cuello de estiércol!

A través de la historia, siempre han existido rinos y siempre han existido vacas. Eso nunca ha cambiado y nunca cambiará. ¡Sólo agradece que tú eres uno de los rinos! Cuando te despiertes en la mañana, agradece que no naciste con un cencerro en tu cuello y el primer sonido que hiciste no fue "muuu."

¡Tú naciste rinoceronte! ¡El primer sonido que hiciste fue un sonoro y estridente rugido de rino! El doctor no tuvo que darte una nalgada para que empezaras a respirar. ¡Naciste motivado! ¡Pagaste la cuenta y saliste de ahí! Tenías que salir para entrar en la jungla y poner tu cuerno sobre algo de inmediato.

UN NEGOCIO PUEDE SER FORMATIVO

¿Ya pusiste tu propio negocio? No hay nada malo en trabajar para otros si tú lo disfrutas, pero si no te gusta, ¿porqué no mejor trabajar para ti mismo? ¡Estamos jugando el juego de la libre empresa! ¿No quieres jugar? Nada se compara con la emoción y la aventura de ser un empresario. Estoy convencido de que habría menos abuso de drogas y alcohol si más animales pusieran su propio negocio.

Míralo de esta manera: drogarte y poner un negocio, ambas opciones conllevan un riesgo, ¿cierto?

"¡Naciste siendo rinoceronte! El doctor no tuvo que darte una nalgada para que empezaras a respirar."

De hecho, si quieres ser atrevido, la actividad empresarial es más arriesgada que las drogas. Con tu propio negocio, puedes ser demasiado por todo lo que vales, puedes ir a la bancarrota, ser acosado por el gobierno, ser robado por tus propios empleados, o por tus clientes, desarrollar úlceras, ser desalojado de tu oficina, que tu inventario se vuelva obsoleto, o simplemente ser aniquilado por la competencia. ¿Te parece que son suficientes emociones?

Con drogas y alcohol, lo peor que puede pasarte es que una sobredosis te cause la muerte. ¡Entonces se acaba todo! ¡Ya no hay más emoción! Esto no sucede con tu negocio. Puedes ir a la quiebra pero la emoción continúa. Tus acreedores, como demonios, seguirán persiguiéndote. El gobierno seguirá enviándote su colección de formas fiscales para ser llenadas. ¡Una demanda legal podría durar años! Lo ves, los negocios son un asunto muy riesgoso. ¡Las drogas ni siquiera se les comparan!

Tal vez los niños se droguen para sentirse bien. Bueno, ¿qué tan bien puede sentirse el convertir tu cerebro y tu cuerpo en una masa blanda? Manejar tu propio negocio, por otro lado, estimula tus terminales nerviosas en lugar de adormecerlas. No hay nada como la emoción de crear algo de la nada.

Las drogas no pueden provocarte el sentimiento eufórico que te da el lograr tus metas, el enfrentar los riesgos y salir airoso, el mal pasarte en la jungla, donde la supervivencia del más fuerte es la regla, y después de todo esto triunfar. Una vez que hayas saboreado la victoria en la jungla, quedarás atado. Nunca podrás volver a trabajar para alguien más.

Para terminar, ¡las drogas te cuestan dinero, mientras que tu negocio te dará dinero! Con tu propio negocio obtienes todos los beneficios de ser atrevido y sentirte bien al mismo tiempo, y además de todo eso, es muy probable que te vuelvas rico en el proceso! ¡Conviértete en un adicto a la libre empresa!

DEJA VOLAR TU MENTE

Con el tiempo tu pequeño negocio ya no te satisfará. Anhelarás más emociones, más riesgos, más estímulos, y empezarás a experimentar con formas más atrevidas del negocio. La presión de los amigos te comprometerá para asociarte con otras corporaciones. Pasarás mayor tiempo con personajes indeseables de la jungla, tales como abogados y contadores. Antes de que te des cuenta de lo que ha sucedido, estarás invistiendo en proyectos de bienes raíces y muchas otras inversiones deducibles de impuesto.

Vastas extensiones de tierra se desarrollarán bajo tu control, tu empresa empleará a miles de animales mientras tu cuenta bancaria crece y tu madre se preguntará qué hizo mal. ¡ESTÁS ATRAPADO! ¡Eres un empresario! ¡ADMÍTELO! Ése es el primer paso hacia la certeza de que SEGUIRÁS así. La jungla es tuya para que la explotes. Nunca volverás a trabajar para otra persona una vez que te des cuenta de eso. Lo siento, Mamá.

"Pasarás mayor tiempo con personajes indeseables de la jungla, tales como abogados y contadores..."

Capítulo 8

UN SAFARI EMPRESARIAL

Ya decidiste aventurarte solo en la jungla. ¡Felicidades! Espero que tu principal razón no sea el dinero. El dinero es demasiado listo para eso. En el momento en que te vea venir, desaparece. Tu safari será frustrante y poco satisfactorio. En vez de eso, ve por diversión. ¡Ve a ver qué puedes hacer y a divertirte como nunca! Disfruta la cacería, goza de la vista y atraparás al dinero sin que se dé cuenta. Si sólo vas por el dinero, estás expuesto a meterte en algo que no te gusta en realidad... como peluquear perros.

Escogí el campo editorial porque me gusta escribir. El arte de la promoción y la publicidad también me atraen y me dan la oportunidad de hablar frente a grupos de personas, lo cual también me gusta. Si no gano un millón de dólares, no me importará porque me divertiré. Prefiero ser feliz y estar quebrado que ser rico y sentirme desgraciado, si es que tuviera que elegir. Claro que ser feliz y rico es lo mejor, y si empiezas con algo que disfrutas, el dinero vendrá a ti.

LOS INGREDIENTES NECESARIOS

Hay tres elementos básicos que constituyen el safari empresarial. Son estos tres elementos los que permiten que el sistema capitalista sea tan exitoso y si tú puedes aprender a combinar estos tres elementos con habilidad, serás capaz de grandes cosas. Estos son *dinero, energía e ideas*. Virtualmente todos los grandes inventos, logros y productos han surgido a través del uso experto de estos tres ingredientes. Pueden trabajar juntos para construir negocios, crear grandes riquezas y, si se aplican correctamente, pueden hacer tu vida muy placentera.

LA FALTA DE "RINO" ES LA RAÍZ DE TODO MAL

El dinero es con mucho el más poderoso de estos tres ingredientes. Si tienes mucho dinero, siempre puedes comprar la energía y las ideas de otros. Por cierto, ¿sabías que la palabra "rino" significa "dinero"? ¡Es cierto! ¡Búscala en tu diccionario si no me crees!

Si no tienes suficiente "rino," no te preocupes. De los tres ingredientes, el dinero es el único que no es natural. Todos nacemos con energía e ideas, pero nadie nace con dinero. Así como el dinero puede comprar energía e ideas, así también las buenas ideas y una energía dirigida apropiadamente pueden conseguir dinero.

TEN ENERGÍA FELIZ

La energía es otro requisito importante en un safari empresarial exitoso. La energía se obtiene más fácilmente cuando haces lo que te gusta. Si amas lo que haces, naturalmente tendrás energía para hacerlo. ¿Cuando vas a esquiar, te quedas en la cama en la mañana temiendo levantarte y tener que ir a esquiar a esas tontas montañas? ¡Claro que no! ¡Llegas temprano a la fila para comprar tu boleto para subir aún antes de que abran! ¿Y regresas temprano, antes de que los elevadores cierren? ¡Por supuesto que no! Corres arriba y abajo tratando de esquiar lo más que puedas durante el día. ¡Después no puedes esperar hasta el día siguiente! Esa es la manera como debes correr a tu negocio para poder tener éxito, así que asegúrate de estar en al campo que más te interese.

Finalmente, debes tener buenas ideas. Todo lo que existe hoy fue alguna vez sólo una idea. ¡Quién sabe qué podría existir dentro de un año, debido a una idea que pueda surgir dentro de ti! Si puedes pensar, puedes imaginar. ¡Y si puedes imaginar, entonces eres creativo!

No olvides que el dinero es solamente una idea. No tiene valor intrínseco. El dinero meramente representa bienes y servicios. Esa fue una gran idea, ¿cierto? Con tus propias ideas brillantes, puedes pensar en algún medio para obtener algo de ese papel sin valor. Más vale que lo hagas. ¿Qué otra cosa estás haciendo que sea tan importante y que no pueda esperar? Mientras estás aquí, ¿por qué no te diviertes y juegas el juego?

LOS VERDADEROS GANADORES

El dinero puede usarse para llevar un marcador aunque los verdaderos ganadores son aquéllos que se divirtieron mientras obtuvieron el dinero. Sin duda, tú tendrás mucho dinero, si es que aún no lo tienes. Tienes ideas y energía lo cual te permitirá obtener tu primer fajo de "rino" y después combinarás ese dinero para crear más dinero. El ciclo continuará hasta que seas inmensamente rico. Entonces tendrás que recordar que debes mantener todo en la perspectiva adecuada.

Dios nos dijo que no atesoraramos cosas en la tierra porque Él sabía que no durarían. Él dijo que las polillas y el moho las consumirían, y los ladrones se meterían y las robarían. ¿Cómo sabía Él eso? Eso es exactamente lo que sucede, y si no te lo esperas, te puedes frustrar.

DA UN PASEO POR EL MUNDO

Ten en mente que tu próspero negocio y todas tus posesiones materiales son meramente piezas temporales en el juego de la vida. Este juego se parece mucho a jugar al Monopolio. Podrías poner hoteles en todas tus propiedades, podrías poseer todas las líneas de ferrocarril, y justo en ese momento, todos los demás jugadores podrían decidir que ya es tarde e irse a su casa porque se tienen que levantar temprano al día siguiente.

Todo el dinero del juego se devuelve al banco y las tarjetas de propiedades, las casas y los hoteles se lanzan dentro de la caja. El juego se ha terminado. ¿Cómo te sentirías? ¡GRANDIOSO! ¡Porque tú ibas ganando! Tú sabías que el juego eventualmente se acabaría pero eso no te hizo dejar de jugar para ganar. ¿Cómo te habrías sentido si hubieras ido perdiendo? ¿Y qué si hubieras caído en la propiedad más cara que pertenecía a otro jugador, y que además tuviera un hotel en ella? ¡Tú habrías sido quien sugiriera que se estaba haciendo tarde! Seguro, era temporal. Pero eso no significa que no debas hacer tu mejor esfuerzo. El triunfo personal siempre es mejor que la derrota temporal. Podrías pasarte la vida en tu safari empresarial construyendo una gran propiedad y después ser golpeado por el torpedo que lleva tu nombre. Pero eso está bien. Ibas ganando y llevabas una vida productiva. Mejor eso, que llevar una vida de perdedor y de hecho estar esperando que llegue ese torpedo y te golpee.

Cuando vas de vacaciones a Hawaii, no te sientas en la habitación del hotel sintiéndote abatido porque sabes que las vacaciones no pueden durar para siempre. No, tú te vas a la playa y disfrutas del tiempo que estarás ahí.

REDISTRIBUCIÓN DE UN MERCEDES

Dios dijo que los ladrones se meterían a tu casa a robar. Así que si se roban tu Mercedes diesel nuevecito, no te preocupes. ¡Puedes comprar otro! Es mejor que los ladrones independientes se lo lleven a que las supervacas del gobierno te lo expropien. Por lo menos los ladrones tienen que trabajar para obtenerlo. El gobierno simplemente te lo quitaría a modo de impuestos. Por lo menos los ladrones disfrutarían del fruto de su trabajo. El gobierno trataría de redistribuirlo. Por lo menos los ladrones ganarían dinero del robo, mientras que el gobierno perdería dinero al tener que pagar para redistribuirlo. ¡Deja que los ladrones se lo lleven! De cualquier modo ya te habías cansado del color.

Disfruta de tus recompensas materiales aquí en la tierra mientras las tengas, sin embargo recuerda que todo es temporal. Tu verdadero tesoro está en el cielo, cuando el juego termine aquí en la tierra. ¡Pero sube como un ganador, no como un perdedor!

Capítulo 9

LA REVOLUCIÓN RINOCERÓNTICA

¡Cuídense supervacas! ¡Nosotros los rinos hemos soportado sus políticas socialistas lo suficiente! Sus abundantes pasturas están creando una inquietante agitación entre aquéllos que viven en la jungla. Las reglas y normas que ustedes arrojan están llegando al límite de la tolerancia de todos los animales para acceder a tal sometimiento. Hasta algunas de las vacas están ahora cuestionando los beneficios de tener a la Vaca Hermana Mayor gobernando sus vidas. La siguiente carta de Linda Timmons enviada al "Times de Los Angeles" el 22 de febrero de 1979 expresa el sentir de muchos.

"Me ha atacado el blues del cheque de pago, y esto me ha hecho pensar en América, tierra de los hombres libres. Siempre había interpretado esa frase como que yo era libre para vivir mi vida como mejor me parezca. Yo creía que tenía el derecho de tomar todas las decisiones que afectaran mi vida siempre y cuando no dañara a los demás o fuera en contra de la ley. Yo creía que las leyes estaban ahí para protegerme, y que las personas que las violaban eran criminales.

Estos conceptos siempre me sonaron bien. Estaba segura que podría llevar una vida feliz y productiva dentro de sus reglas, porque yo sabía que una persona honesta, consciente y responsable de mis actos. Yo estaba orgullosa de ser americana.

Viví en esta fantasía hasta que cumplí 19 años. Fue entonces que mi esposo recibió ese aviso de reclutamiento, en nuestro primer aniversario de bodas. En unos días el chico que amaba desde que tenía trece años se había ido. El gobierno que hizo las leyes para protegerme, dijo que él tenía que ir donde se le mandara y que tenía que hacer lo que le ordenaban. Si no lo hacía, él sería un criminal y podría ir a la cárcel. Y entonces lo enviaron a Vietnam. Ellos pusieron su vida en riesgo sin su consentimiento. Yo no lo entendía.

Mi esposo regresó sano y salvo 11 meses después, y fue licenciado con honores del servicio. Iniciamos una familia, ahorramos dinero y compramos una casita en Hermosa Beach, donde los dos habíamos crecido. Tuvimos cuidado de no endeudarnos. Cada año los impuestos del predial de nuestra casita se incrementaban; en 1976 se duplicaron y el año pasado se duplicaron de nuevo. No podíamos pagar los 2,400 dólares que el gobierno quería —pero ésta era nuestra casita, este era el pueblo donde crecimos. ¿Qué podíamos hacer? El gobierno, que hacía las leyes para protegernos, dijo que teníamos que pagar si queríamos quedarnos. No lo entendía.

La propuesta 13 rebajó los impuestos de nuestra propiedad, y así pudimos conservar nuestra casa. Sin embargo ahora la Corte está sugiriendo que mis hijos tal vez no puedan seguir asistiendo a la escuela que está en la esquina de nuestra calle; tal vez tengan que ir en autobús y tardar 45 minutos de ida y 45 minutos de regreso, para ir a la escuela en otro pueblo. Nosotros elegimos vivir en este pueblo porque crecimos aquí. Es una comunidad pequeña, con muchos ciudadanos comprometidos. Queríamos que nuestros hijos se enorgullecieran de su comunidad y de su escuela. El gobierno, que hace reglas para protegernos, dice que esto no es importante; algo llamado integración (no educación) es más importante.

El hecho de recibir lo que quedaba de impuestos de mis primeros cheques de paga de 1979 me ha hecho reflexionar sobre mi vida. Creo que finalmente comprendo: no soy libre en lo absoluto; el gobierno es el que es libre para hacer lo que quiera. Las leyes no son hechas para proteger a mi familia y a mi; son hechas para proteger al gobierno con nuestro dinero, nuestros niños, –nuestras mismas vidas. Si no lo hacemos, nos arriesgamos a violar la ley.

Sí, ahora entiendo, y ya no estoy tan segura de cómo me siento respecto de ser una persona honesta, consciente y responsable de mis actos. América, la tierra de los hombres libres –me suena hueco. Todavía me siento orgullosa de ser Americana, y no me gustaría vivir en ningún otro lado, pero ya no soy tan ingenua como antes".

¡La rebelión ha comenzado! La victoria aplastante del Presidente Reagan sobre Jimmy Carter en 1980 marcó el comienzo. El mensaje de la jungla es claro: ¡líbrate de las supervacas! El Rino Ronald Reagan fue el primer presidente en mucho tiempo que prometió a la población de la jungla menos... menos gobierno, menos reglas y menos impuestos.

LOS PRINCIPIOS BÁSICOS DE LA REBELIÓN

Regresemos 20 años a la década de los sesentas. ¿Recuerdas a los hippies? Los animados jóvenes que crecían en esa época se rebelaron contra el sistema. Ahora bien, no hay nada malo en protestar, ¿cierto? La rebeldía es una parte natural del crecimiento. La parte difícil es encontrar algo por lo que protestar y el blanco más fácil de atacar es cualquier cosa en lo que tus padres crean. Los padres nunca están en onda, ya sabes.

En los sesentas los padres no creían en el amor libre, ¡así que esto era lo apropiado! Los padres creían en que sólo las niñas debían traer el pelo largo, así que de repente, los chicos debían traerlo. Ningún padre quería que sus hijos fumaran marihuana, así que obviamente se hizo muy popular. ¿Captas la idea? Cualquier cosa que tus padres *quieran* que hagas, tú *no quieres* hacerlo, y cualquier cosa que ellos *no quieren* que hagas, tú *real-*

mente quieres hacerlo. Eso es rebeldía en pocas palabras.

NO CONFÍES EN NADIE MAYOR DE TREINTA AÑOS

Ahora mira lo que ha sucedido. Los niños de las flores, los hippies y los yippies de los sesentas están llegando ahora a la edad de ser padres. ¡Muchos de ellos ya tienen 30 años! ¡Recuerda que nosotros los niños no confiamos en nadie mayor de treinta años!

Estos niños de los sesentas están asumiendo la dirección del sistema y ganando poder donde antes no tenían ninguno. Puedes encontrarlos enseñando sus puntos de vista liberales en escuelas, hay muchos publicando sus opiniones en libros, periódicos, la televisión y el cine. Cientos de miles de ellos están trabajando en el gobierno, algunos están aspirando a puestos de poder para asegurarse de que vivamos del modo que ellos creen que deberíamos vivir. Su objetivo parece ser hacer la vida de todos fácil y libre de riesgos. Ellos promueven el control de armas, la convivencia de diferentes clases sociales entre escolares, la igualdad, el control de precios, desayunos escolares gratis, más beneficencia, acabar con las plantas nucleares, leyes de cinturones de seguridad en los autos, etc...

NUEVA OLA DE DESCONTENTO

Pero, ¿adivina qué? Los niños de los sesentas son ahora padres, y los niños de los ochentas empiezan a rebelarse. Compara a los punks de ahora con los hippies de los sesentas. Los hippies llevaban el pelo y la barba largos y descuidados. Ahora el estilo es pelo muy corto a veces con rayos de colores brillantes, y absolutamente nada de pelo facial. Los hippies usaban jeans acampanados y los punks llevan pantalones de tubo. Los hippies cantaban acerca del amor libre y la paz. La música "new wave" de ahora está llena de violencia. Las drogas suaves de los sesentas son reemplazadas por drogas más violentas y peligrosas como el PCP o bien, la tendencia ahora es no usar drogas en absoluto.

Está ocurriendo una revuelta definitiva. Es la Revolución Rinoceróntica y está rápidamente cambiando las costumbres en la jungla. El liberalismo de los sesentas está ahora sucumbiendo ante el conservadurismo de Reagan el cual muy pronto se combinará con la libertad económica de los ochentas y los noventas.

LA LIBRE EMPRESA DEL LAISSEZ-FAIRE

Más que pelear por apoyo para enterrar la seguridad como hacía la vieja generación, nuestra generación luchará por una forma de capitalismo de laissez-faire. Laissez-faire, significa "una doctrina que se opone a la intervención gubernamental en los asuntos económicos más allá de lo necesario para mantener la paz y los derechos de propiedad." En otras palabras, la nueva generación NO aceptará ningún tipo de gobierno, excepto el que exista para proteger las vidas y propiedades de todos los animales de Las Junglas Unidas de América.

Esto te puede sonar terrible ahora y es por eso que la joven generación luchará por ello. El pelo largo en los hombres solía escandalizar. Los Beatles solían escandalizar. No olvides los fundamentos de la *rebeldía:* cualquier cosa que *ellos* no quieran, *nosotros lo queremos*, y viceversa.

OPORTUNIDADES RINOCERÓNTICAS

Otra razón para esta tendencia hacia el capitalismo del laissez-faire es el hecho de que habrá nuevas y grandiosas oportunidades que se presentarán durante la Revolución Rinoceróntica y nadie tolerará que ninguna supervaca retrase las cosas con sus reglas y normas. Nuevas y fantásticas tecnologías están emergiendo con la promesa de nuevas fortunas, y nadie estará dispuesto a aceptar que le impongan ningún tipo de impuestos que sirvan para costear burocracias estorbosas.

Las fortunas hechas por rinos como J. Paul Getty con el petróleo durante la primera parte de este siglo serán duplicadas, pero no con petróleo. ¡El petróleo, el gas y el carbón ya van de salida, se están acabando! Nadie pensó en regresar algo del petróleo al subsuelo así que cada vez es mas difícil encontrarlo. Y los desatinados burócratas han envuelto a la industria completa con papeles burocráticos y normas diversas que hacen que la exploración de nuevas fuentes de petróleo sea prohibitiva o imposible debido al costo.

Sólo para mostrarte cómo piensan las supervacas, ¿sabías que los burócratas han creado un Departamento de Energía con aproximadamente 20,000 empleados que nunca han producido un kilovatio de energía? ¡Ni siquiera una sola gota de petróleo! Todo lo que han hecho es restringir la producción y distribución del petróleo, una noble meta para una agencia gubernamental. ¡Oye, olvídalo! El petróleo pronto será obsoleto de todos modos. ¡Afortunadamente, también lo será el gobierno!

Conforme nuevas y más eficientes fuentes de energía se desarrollen, ¿crees que vamos a permitir que las supervacas pongan sus patas sobre ellas y que confundan las cosas otra vez? ¡De ninguna manera! Si va a crearse alguna agencia, ésta será el Departamento de la Burocracia, ¡cuyo propósito será restringir la producción y distribución de supervacas! ¡Piensa en todo el dinero que esta agencia podría ahorrarnos!

El futuro está en nuevas fuentes de energía que sean inagotables y que no contaminen. ¡La gran raza está decidida a encontrar y desarrollar nuevos tipos de energía en la jungla! ¡Tú podrías ser parte de ellos y ganar millones de dólares! Observa la tecnología solar, la geotérmica y el desarrollo del hidrógeno. Todo se ha probado ahora y la frenética carrera está en camino. La fuerza de las olas, los desechos del coco, y hasta prender fuegos artificiales se ha intentado para suministrar una fuente de energía que no se agote.

CANCHAS NUCLEARES DE BALÓN MANO

La tecnología nuclear no será la fuente de energía más importante tampoco por tres razones. La primera es que el gobierno ayudó a iniciarla, lo que nos dice que probablemente no la necesitamos.

En segundo lugar, los reactores nucleares necesitan uranio y ¿qué pasará cuando se acabe el uranio? Yo nunca he estado dentro de un reactor nuclear, ¡pero desde afuera parecen unas canchas de balón mano!

En tercer lugar, producen desechos tóxicos. Las nuevas fuentes de energía no generarán desechos, o utilizarán sus propios desechos para producir más energía. Sin embargo cualquier riesgo o peligro potencial de la energía nuclear NO es la razón para descartarla. La vida en la jungla siempre tendrá riesgos. Las vacas simplemente no pueden meterse eso en sus cabezas. De hecho, si la permanencia de la tecnología nuclear ayudara a que el gobierno protegiera nuestra libertad contra los animales salvajes, lo cual era desde el principio el motivo por el cual fue instituido, yo estaría con ellos.

Obviamente los rusos no están interesados en retrasar su crecimiento nuclear. Nosotros queremos evitar que el gobierno se meta en nuestras vidas, ¡pero no dejemos que los rusos lo hagan por nosotros! Necesitamos la tecnología nuclear como un freno a la agresión en contra de Las Junglas Unidas de América, pero busquemos otras fuentes de

"Yo nunca he estado dentro de un reactor nuclear, pero desde afuera parecen canchas de balón mano"

energía para operar nuestros aparatos eléctricos de masaje para cuernos y para encender nuestras podadoras de césped. Tenemos que mantener el pasto corto para evitar atraer a las vacas, quienes podrían pensar que han encontrado un lugar para pastar.

LA JUNGLA COMPUTARIZADA

Mientras Henry Ford hizo su fortuna con autos, los rinos de la Revolución Rinoceróntica estarán amasando su gran fortuna a través de la proliferación de las computadoras. En 1979, de acuerdo con la revista "Computer World", "Si la industria automotriz hubiera hecho lo que la industria de las computadoras ha hecho en los últimos 30 años, un Rolls-Royce costaría dos dólares con cincuenta centavos y daría dos millones de millas por galón de gasolina."

¡Muy pronto cada hogar en la jungla tendrá una computadora! ¡Serán tan comunes como los excusados! ¿Puedes imaginarte el dinero que se ganará en esta industria? ¡Es excitante! Muchas fortunas se harán del desarrollo, manufactura, distribución, reparación y venta de computadoras para el hogar.

La década del empresario de computadoras está aquí mientras la industria electrónica invade la jungla. Tu auto muy pronto podrá hablarte y tú te comunicarás con el mundo exterior a través de tu terminal de computadora. ¡Tal cual podría eventualmente eliminar la necesidad de que nuestro gobierno opere el Sistema Postal! Tu casa electrónica se encargará de todo, desde llamar al plomero para que arregle la tubería, hasta de despertarte en la mañana. ¡Hasta tendremos vacas electrónicas algún día! Las vacas no están muy felices con ello, y ésta es otra razón por la que las vacas no sonríen.

GENÉTICA DE LA JUNGLA

Al principio de este siglo, muchas fortunas tales como las de Andrew Carnegie fueron hechas en la industria del acero, la ingeniería genética sostiene la misma promesa durante la Revolución Rinoceróntica. Una ciencia relativamente nueva, la industria biológica, creará muchas oportunidades en los próximos años conforme se vayan haciendo nuevos descubrimientos. Alvin Toffler en su libro "La Tercera Ola" publica que los científicos "están estudiando la idea de utilizar bacterias capaces de convertir la luz solar en energía electroquímica." Toffler también sugiere que "la biología reducirá o eliminará la necesidad del petróleo en la producción de plásticos, fertilizantes, ropa, pintura, pesticidas y miles de productos más." Él dice que "la ingeniería genética será empleada para aumentar las reservas mundiales de alimentos."

¡Wow! Entre la demanda de nuevas fuentes de energía, dominio de las computadoras y el desarrollo de la ingeniería genética, la jungla será un lugar muy ocupado. ¡Vas a tener que ser un rino para estar a la altura! ¡Olvídate de preocuparte por los buitres y los bichos que te pican, cuando empieces a ir más lento... por ahora lo que debe preocuparte es ser reemplazado por una computadora, o ser alterado biológicamente.

LOS POLÍTICOS:
UNA ESPECIE EN EXTINCIÓN

Conforme los rinos jóvenes y revolucionarios de hoy y del mañana empiezan a involucrarse en estas nuevas y emocionantes industrias, mientras se rebelan en contra de las opiniones liberales de la nueva generación de adultos maduros, la tendencia hacia el sistema de la libre empresa del laissez-faire comenzará. A diferencia del niño de las flores de antaño, la nueva generación pugnará por el individualismo, la independencia y el deseo de enfrentar los retos y arriesgarse. El gobierno de hoy no fomenta estos ideales y, por lo tanto, será rechazado.

El gobierno inflado, creador de la supervaca, algún día será una historia del pasado. El político de carrera será olvidado, obsoleto y una reliquia en desuso conforme las burocracias se derrumban y caen por su propio peso. La vida en la jungla vibrará de nuevo con el impulso que da el logro de sus objetivos porque el incentivo estará ahí. La oportunidad de mejorar el propio puesto de uno en la jungla (el Sueño Americano) vivirá otra vez y las Junglas Unidas de América seguirán siendo el país más grande del mundo.

"Muy pronto cada hogar en la jungla tendrá su computadora personal"

Capítulo 10

LA EDUCACIÓN DE LA JUNGLA

El último capítulo estuvo bastante pesado ¿cierto? No es mi estilo escribir cosas tan serias, pero siento que es imperativo para el futuro del rino el acabar con el poder de las supervacas. –¡Los rinos están cercanos a su extinción ahora! Si no hacemos algo pronto, los animales del futuro sólo conocerán al rino si nos ven disecados en un museo.

Este libro, estoy seguro, será más controversial que "El Rinoceronte" porque ahora estoy presentando mis puntos de vista acerca de áreas más sensibles. Me doy cuenta de que algunos de mis pensamientos serán rechazados por algunos de mis compañeros rinos y aplaudidos por otros. Yo sé lo que las vacas estarán pensando, lo cual esta bien, porque todos tenemos derecho a tener nuestra propia opinión. Aunque estoy seguro de que algunos me discutirán ese punto también.

NADIE ESTÁ DE ACUERDO CON NADA

El año pasado asistí a un seminario sobre clasificación de correos donde los tres millonarios en este ramo estaban presentes para revelar la supuesta forma apropiada para clasificar el correo para poner y hacer crecer un negocio en ésta área. Estos tipos eran supuestamente los expertos ¿cierto? ¡Yo había pagado para escucharlos!

Bien, desde el principio ninguno estaba de acuerdo con los otros. Uno dijo que usar un Apartado Postal estaba bien, mientras los otros no estaban de acuerdo. Uno admitía mucho texto y lo otros no. Discutieron acerca de productos, etiquetas de correo, anuncios ¡y finalmente discutieron acerca del precio de admisión que se había cobrado para escucharlos!

Yo no aprendí mucho sobre la clasificación del correo, pero sí aprendí sobre el comportamiento animal. Y créeme ¡estos hombres eran animales para cuando el seminario llegó a su fin! Aprendí que no importa lo que opines, SIEMPRE habrá ALGUIEN que no estará de acuerdo. No importa el tema. Sólo junta a expertos en religión y jamás se pondrán de acuerdo. Agrupa a los políticos más importantes del mundo y discutirán. Une a los criadores de pollos más experimentados del mundo y discutirán sobre las técnicas de crianza. ¿Captas la idea? Parece que nadie puede estar de acuerdo con nada, a excepción del desacuerdo y ¡hasta habrá quienes no estén de acuerdo con eso!

MANTÉNTE UNIDO A TU CUERNO

Yo no soy la excepción. ¡Tengo opiniones muy fuertes sobre ciertos asuntos que SE QUE SON LOS CORRECTOS! Nadie me convencerá jamás de lo contrario. "Plántate en tus opiniones" me dice siempre mi abuela. Bien, sabemos que los rinos cargamos con cuernos. Así que manténte unido a tu cuerno (no suena tan bien ¿cierto?). De todos modos, sólo hazlo, no puedo darle gusto a todos. Intentarlo sería sólo una lección frustrante. Los rinos tienen sus propios puntos de vista. No seas como el insensato ganado cuyos cerebros son masas blandas. Piensa por ti mismo. Eres el experto en lo que tú piensas y crees. Nunca dejes que nadie controle eso por ti. Los primeros pasos al socialismo y después al comunismo son controlar la mente de todos.

MATA A LA MULA

Sólo porque todos los demás son vacas no significa que tú tengas que ser vaca también. Esa forma de pensar del "yo también" puede meterte en serios problemas, como dice Billy Martin en su autobiografía titulada "El Número 1." Él recuerda cuando fue a Texas con Mickey Mantle de cacería al rancho de un amigo. Ellos llegaron al rancho después de viajar unas horas y Mickey Mantle entró a la casa para ver al dueño del rancho mientras Billy Martin esperaba afuera en el auto.

El dueño les dio permiso de cazar ahí y le pidió a Mickey un favor. Había una mula vieja que se estaba quedando ciega y el propietario no tenía corazón para matar a la pobre mula, así que le pidió a Mickey que lo hiciera en su lugar. Mickey estuvo de acuerdo en matar a la vieja mula.

De camino afuera, cuando se dirigía al auto donde Billy esperaba, a Mickey se le ocurrió la idea de hacerle una broma a Billy. Saltó dentro del coche, cerró la puerta de golpe, puso cara de enojo y le dijo a Billy que estaba furioso. Billy le preguntó: "¿Qué te pasa?
Mickey respondió, "No nos permitirá cazar aquí y estoy furioso, así que voy a ir al granero y mataré a su mula."
"¡Mickey, tu no puedes matar a su mula!" Billy protestó. Pero Mickey insistió en que nada lo detendría mientras manejaba hacia el corral. Encontraron a la mula y ambos salieron corriendo del coche. Mickey levantó su rifle y le disparó a la vieja mula. Después volteó y vió a Billy con su rifle humeante. "¿Qué estás haciendo?" preguntó Mickey y Billy respondió, "me eché a dos de sus vacas."

UNA ALTERNATIVA A LA UNIVERSIDAD

Otro ejemplo de la forma de pensar del "yo también" es la migración masiva de los chicos que salen de la preparatoria para entrar directamente en la universidad. Mis padres querían que yo también tuviera el mismo obstáculo que todos los demás, así que intentaron enviarme a la universidad también. ¡Sólo bromeaba! No pude resistir la tentación de incluir esta frase aquí

Hablando en serio, me gustaría proponer una alternativa en lugar de correr hacia la universidad, especialmente a los niños que no están bien seguros de lo que quieren hacer en la vida. Por supuesto, si quieres ser doctor, dentista, abogado, maestro o cualquier otra cosa que requiera una educación universitaria, mete la velocidad y ve hacia allá. Si no estás seguro de lo que quieres hacer, pero tienes la oportunidad de ir a la universidad y *si quieres* ir, entonces asegúrate de quedar inscrito.

Pero si planeas ir de mala gana a la universidad sólo porque tus padres quieren que lo hagas, o porque tus amigos van a ir, no desperdicies tu dinero.

Cuando yo salí de la preparatoria, mis padres querían que fuera a la universidad y yo les pregunté por qué. Ellos dijeron, "Para que puedas obtener un mejor empleo." Fue entonces que supe que yo no quería ir a la universidad.

Para mi no hay tal cosa como "un mejor empleo." Yo ya había decidido ser un empresario de la selva. Seguramente no podría conseguirme un empleo seguro, pero si podría dar empleos seguros a otras personas. Alguien tiene que contratar a los universitarios, ¿no crees? Kim y yo, ambos, optamos por la aventura en vez de la seguridad.

CAPITALISMO PARA PRINCIPIANTES

Yo me di cuenta de que no necesitaba ir a la universidad para aprender cómo ser un empresario. Además, no había clases de "capitalismo para principiantes" disponibles en la universidad. Así como la mayoría de las escuelas públicas no alientan a los empresarios, tampoco la mayoría de nuestras universidades enseñan las ventajas de nuestro sistema de libre empresa, aunque eso está empezando a cambiar ahora conforme la Revolución Rinoceróntica va avanzando. De nuevo, existen algunas vacas profesionales involucradas cuyos intereses no se verían beneficiados si se enseña el capitalismo.

William E. Simon, una supervaca que se convirtió en rino (el anterior Secretario del Tesoro), dice que "las universidades más importantes de América están ahora produciendo jóvenes colectivistas por multitudes." Simon en su libro "El Tiempo De La Verdad" explica: "Hubo un tiempo, hace 40 o 50 años, en que el capitalismo *fue* la forma ortodoxa dominante, no sólo en el gobierno y en el mercado, sino en las universidades también. En ese tiempo, se insistía en que era por el bien de la sociedad como unidad que la voz disonante fuera escuchada en esos planteles —que la crítica al capitalismo, el disidente de su filosofía, su economía, sus costumbres y tradiciones fueran escuchadas— y, como siempre, el capitalismo respondió haciendo precisamente eso. De verdad, es a través de la generosidad y tolerancia del capitalismo que sus enemigos han llegado a dominar los planteles universitarios de hoy en día."

Tal vez en algunos años, durante la Revolución Rinoceróntica, cuando los jóvenes rinos se harten de las tendencias socialistas y exijan un cambio hacia el sistema capitalista del laissez-faire, entonces el capitalismo se imponga una vez más como la forma ortodoxa dominante. De hecho, actualmente hay por lo menos cuatro universidades en el país ofreciendo más estudios empresariales.

SIN PENSIÓN ALIMENTICIA

En realidad, el mejor momento para experimentar cómo ser un empresario es justo después de la preparatoria cuando estás joven. Puedes ir a la universidad en cualquier momento de tu vida, pero para poner un negocio necesitas esa tremenda energía que tienes cuando eres joven. Hace poco conocí a un chico de 17 años llamado Scott Mahfouz quien ha estado manejando su propio negocio desde que tenía 14 años. Él inició un negocio de pedidos por correo y de reproducción de cintas. ¡Aún antes de graduarse de la preparatoria ya tenía a sus amigos de la escuela trabajando para él! Ahora está ahorrando dinero para comprarse un Rolls-Royce y espero verlo conduciéndolo por nuestra calle dentro de unos años.

¿Qué mejor momento para empezar tu propio negocio que cuando estás joven y no tienes compromisos familiares? No hay bebés que alimentar (esperamos) y no hay esposo o esposa con quien debas reportarte. Una nota de advertencia: asegúrate de que cuando llegues a casarte, te unas a un rinoceronte AAA certificado, porque no querrás pasarte la vida arrastrando a una vaca tras de ti. Ambos serán miserables. Los matrimonios interculturales pueden ser difíciles. Para evitar frustrarse, las vacas deben casarse con vacas, y los rinos con rinos.

Por lo general, cuando inicialmente sales de la preparatoria, no tienes muchas obligaciones económicas, tales como pagos de hipotecas, el ortodoncista de los niños, y pensión alimenticia para tu ex. Eso te permite invertir todo tu tiempo y energía en un negocio sin morirte de hambre al principio. Tal vez tus padres te dejen vivir con ellos hasta que eches a andar el negocio.

MEGADÓLARES S.A.

Recuerda que no estoy hablando de iniciar una gigantesca corporación de megadólares. Tienes que empezar en pequeño. Hasta podría ser un negocio de medio tiempo mientras vas a la universidad. Yo empecé lavando autos y ayudando a Kim a peluquear poodles. Puedes ir a la biblioteca e investigar en libros que dan información sobre oportunidades de negocios pequeños que puedes iniciar con menos de quinientos dólares, o bien puedes idear algo por ti mismo.

PRUEBA TUS CUERNOS

Cuando eres joven, eres flexible, no tienes compromisos económicos, tienes más energía y generalmente eres más audaz porque en realidad no tienes nada que perder. Cuando nuestra estética de perros fracasó, mis hijos no se murieron de hambre porque no tenía hijos. ¡Mi crédito no fue manchado porque no tenía crédito para empezar! ¡No fui un degradado social porque sólo era un niño!

Tal vez podrías intentar asistir un año a la universidad y después un año probando tus cuernos en la jungla. ¡Haz lo que sientas que es mejor para ti, sólo asegúrate de HACER algo! Y para ustedes los rinos que salieron de la preparatoria hace algunos años, no dejen que eso los desanime a hacer su propio safari empresarial. ¡Tienen la piel más gruesa y aún no están listos para las pasturas!

"Asegúrate de que cuando llegues a casarte, te unas a un rinoceronte AAA certificado"

Capítulo 11

EPÍLOGO

Es sorprendente lo que puedes aprender al leer el diccionario, ¿no es cierto? Aquí hay una palabra interesante con la que topé el otro día –epilimnio. Resulta ser que en cualquier cuerpo de agua caliente hay tres capas. La capa superior, más ligera y caliente y que es rica en oxígeno se llama epilimnio. La siguiente capa es la termoclina. Esta es una capa delgada que separa el epilimnio de la capa inferior, más fría, más pesada, y con menos oxígeno. ¡Ahora me estoy volviendo loco porque no puedo averiguar cómo se llama la capa inferior! Si tú lo sabes, mucho apreciaría que me enviaras una postal para informarme.

De todos modos, para no salirme tanto del tema, justo después de la palabra "epilimnio", me encontré con la palabra "Epílogo" –"una sección que concluye y completa la idea de un trabajo literario." De inmediato pensé, "¡Eso es lo que *tengo* que tener en mi libro!" Ahora aquí está. ¡Lo estás leyendo! Y pensar que el mes pasado sólo era una palabra más en el diccionario. Como que se sienten escalofríos por todo el cuerpo, ¿no es cierto?

ESCALOFRÍOS DE EMOCIÓN

Me dan escalofríos, sin embargo no estoy seguro de que se deban a que he dado vida a un epílogo. Creo que mis escalofríos son más bien estremecimientos de pensar en cómo algunos animales de la selva reaccionarán al leer este libro... tales como mi Papá, quien trabaja para el gobierno. ¿Cómo se sentirá de haber sido etiquetado como supervaca? ¿Y qué hay de los padres de Kim, ya que ambos fueron a la universidad y creen firmemente que la educación universitaria es altamente recomendable? Ellos probablemente no me volverán a dirigir la palabra después de leer mi teoría de "la universidad puede ser peligrosa para tu salud."

Tal vez los escalofríos se conviertan en estremecimientos de imaginar la respuesta del gobierno a "Rinocerología Avanzada." Ahora estaré expuesto a que Hacienda, la CIA y el FBI intenten meterme a la cárcel por tratar de derrocar al gobierno. ¿Cómo se sentirá el pastor de nuestra iglesia cuando vea a Dios ilustrado como un rinoceronte? ¡Podría ser excomulgado! Mis estremecimientos podrían deberse a la idea de tener a los líderes de los sindicatos tras de mí por crear inquietudes laborales. ¿Y qué hay si TODO EL MUNDO renuncia a su empleo y NADIE se presenta a trabajar mañana? ¡Podría estar en problemas!

¿CÓMO SUCEDIÓ ESTO?

En realidad yo sólo empecé con la idea de que escribiría otro simple librito motivacional para que siguiera a "El Rinoceronte." No sé qué pasó. Empiezo inocentemente con la premisa de que hay una jungla allá afuera, y de alguna forma, terminé enemistándome con todo mi mercado. ¿Ahora quién comprará el libro? Ciertamente he eliminado a muchos compradores potenciales con mis sugerencias sobre la necesidad de recortar a la burocracia. "Rinocerología Avanzada" definitivamente no estará en la lista de lecturas para todos los trabajadores del servicio civil. ¿Qué clase de compañía va a distribuir mi libro entre sus empleados y arriesgarse a que les renuncien para iniciar sus propias empresas? ¿Qué pastor de la Iglesia recomendará mi libro cuando me refiero a Dios como "tu guía para el safari"?

La "Rinocerología Avanzada" sin duda será prohibido en todos los colegios y universidades y es probable que los empleados postales se rehusen a entregar nada con mi nombre en él. ¿Cómo sucedió todo esto? Hasta mi querido Papá, a quien amo tanto, probablemente tirará a la basura su ejemplar de cortesía y después vaciará los restos de café encima.

Bueno, ¡nadie dijo que sería fácil!

RECUERDA QUE LA VIDA ES UNA AVENTURA. ¡VE Y VÍVELA!

ACERCA DEL AUTOR

Scott Alexander es un rinoceronte (de la especie ceratotherium simum). A menudo visto en Laguna Hills, California, es más que nada activo en la mañana y en la tarde. Aunque es un animal solitario, Scott es visto en ocasiones revolcándose en el fango con su bella esposa, Kimber (también de la especie ceratotherium simum). Con un peso de 2,785 kilogramos, Scott trota a una velocidad de 30 kilómetros por hora, pero puede llegar a correr a 40 kilómetros por hora cuando es presionado. Se alimenta totalmente de pasto, y reportes confiables indican que el cuerno de Scott media más de un metro de largo.

Esta obra se terminó de imprimien
los talleres de Planeta Press S.A. de C.V.
Av. San Nicolás Tolentino No. 279-39
Col. San Nicolás Tolentino 09850
el tiro fue de 1000 ejemplares

INTELLIGENT PRAYER

By the same Author
 THE TEACHING OF
       JESUS ON PRAYER
 HOW TO PRAY FOR HEALING

INTELLIGENT PRAYER

by

LEWIS MACLACHLAN
M.A.

Foreword by
REV. CANON L. W. GRENSTED, D.D.
*Nolloth Professor of the Philosophy of the
Christian Religion in the University
of Oxford*

JAMES CLARKE & CO., LTD.
33, STORE STREET,
LONDON, W.C.1

First published in 1946
Second impression February 1947
Third impression October 1947
Fourth impression January 1950
Fifth impression Jannary 1951
Sixth impression November 1951
Seventh impression October 1952
Eighth impression November 1953
Ninth impression September 1954
Tenth impression October 1955
Eleventh impression December 1956
Twelfth impression April 1958
Thirteenth impression April 1960
Fourteenth impression May 1962

Printed in Great Britain by
The Camelot Press Ltd., London and Southampton

CONTENTS

FOREWORD	.	7
I. AN ART TO BE LEARNT	.	9
II. APPEARANCE AND REALITY	.	12
III. PRAYER IS CONTROLLED THINKING	.	15
IV. THE POWER OF THOUGHT	.	18
V. READJUSTMENT TO LIFE	.	22
VI. HOW TO PRAY	.	27
VII. IS TROUBLE SENT BY GOD?	.	32
VIII. DOES GOD PUNISH US?	.	35
IX. DO WE GET OUR DESERTS?	.	38
X. PRAYING FOR HEALTH	.	41
XI. REASONS FOR UNANSWERED PRAYER	.	46
XII. PRAYER IS OBEDIENCE TO NATURAL LAW	.	51
XIII. HOW TO PRAY FOR HEALING	.	54
XIV. OBJECTIONS TO PRAYER FOR HEALING	.	58
XV. TWO KINDS OF SUFFERING	.	65
XVI. PRAYER FOR CHANGE OF CHARACTER	.	71
XVII. DEALING WITH OUR OWN FAULTS FIRST	.	75
XVIII. AN INTERCESSION FOR THE SICK OF SOUL	.	80
XIX. PRAYER FOR CHRISTIAN WORK	.	83
XX. PRAYER FOR PROSPERITY	.	87
XXI. FAITH AND FINANCE	.	91
XXII. PRAYER FOR PROTECTION	.	94
XXIII. IS PRAYER SELFISH?	.	99

FOREWORD

"PRAYER is the soul's sincere desire, Uttered or unexpressed." There are few better known definitions of prayer than these lines, and obviously it is a profound truth that every deep and sincere craving of the human spirit is in fact addressed to God, and heard and answered by God. Yet those who so easily sing James Montgomery's hymn are often quite unaware that they are taking prayer for granted, without considering either the need for thinking about its true character or the even greater need for such exercise in prayer as may lead to its full development. For those consequences flow at once from the fact that our deep and sincere cravings are, as such, simply cravings of human spirits sorely in need of regeneration and enlightenment. If, to quote a still more famous definition, prayer is to be regarded as "the ascent of the mind to God," then very clearly we shall need to learn something of the stages of the ascent, the steps of the *Scala Perfectionis*, and we shall need too to discipline that mind which is to seek its Maker, not only by praying, but also by thinking as we pray, until our thought and our prayer are one.

For prayer is as easy as the first cry of a child, demanding its mother's attention, and as profound and difficult as the last question asked by a philosopher of this strange mystery which constitutes our world. Very often it happens that those who have learned to pray as children continue to pray as children all their lives, and never realise that it is just as natural for the children of God to grow up in their praying as it is for the children of men to grow up in their physical bodies. If, indeed, we fail to grow up something has gone amiss. And then if difficulties come, if prayer seems to be unanswered or we pass through the desert of dryness, so well known to the saints, our prayer-life is in danger of vanishing altogether.

It is for that reason that I want to welcome and to commend this little book, in which the practice of the life of prayer and the discussion of its problems go hand in hand, as they should. Its inspiration is drawn, as I have reason to know, not only from an individual experience of praying but also from that of a group studying and practising intercession together. In particular, the ancient Christian belief that prayer does avail for healing is seen not merely as a problem, but as the working out of the full significance of what the Christian means when he speaks of God. Treated at the purely intellectual level, it is most certainly a problem, or even a foolish side-tracking of the rational human spirit. But at the level of faith in God, revealed in Jesus Christ, the problem is transformed into a quest, in which the love of man seeks and finds wholly rational the response of the love of God to his seeking.

Mind, feeling, will—all are involved. It is probably the mind that is most often forgotten in our praying, and that is one of the reasons why our prayer-life often runs so very thin. Perhaps the chief merit of this study, after its sincerity, is that it does seek to correct the balance and to give thinking its due and proper place in relation to our prayers.

L. W. GRENSTED.

ORIEL COLLEGE,
OXFORD.

I

AN ART TO BE LEARNT

DOES Prayer make any difference? Some kinds of prayer do not. In the interests of truth, that is to say, in the interest of true religion, it must be said frankly that what is often called prayer makes very little difference to anybody. Perfunctory prayers, casual and vague entreaties to an unknown God, occasional acts of patronage to the Almighty, do as much good as make-believe usually does.

What is not so often observed, and needs some explanation, is the fact that anxious and fearful prayers, though they certainly are not without effect, do more harm than good. Perhaps most prayer is of this kind, for people who pray at no other time will pray when they are in trouble. They are right to pray, but the fact that they pray in fear and not in faith makes the prayer futile or even harmful.[1]

Some good people, speaking for the sake of edification and not from a scientific regard for facts, would say that selfish prayers are never answered. Curiously enough, however, many quite selfish prayers do have very important if not always very desirable results. This is because prayer, like other mental phenomena, is controlled and conditioned by laws of Nature which invariably operate. It is possible for us to use them, or misuse them, or even disuse them, but they are present in life and never fail to respond to our advances.

This all-important fact about prayer is ignored by those who never pray because they think it must be useless or even wrong to do so, except as a spiritual exercise, and, the only sort of prayer they know being that learned in

---

[1] Of course they ought not to stop praying but continue to pray until they obtain the promised peace of mind. Phil. iv. 6-7.

infancy, it does not exercise the spirit to any great extent. Such people never pray, not because they do not believe in God, but because they believe in God so much. "Surely," they say, "God has fixed everything in perfect wisdom and in perfect love. Who am I that I should attempt to alter it?" It must be absurd, they think, to suppose that human wishes can make any difference to the immutable laws of Nature by which the whole universe is governed, and even if we could somehow change the course of events by some occult process, it would be very foolish and impious to try to impose our own ignorant wills on the eternal will of God. This belief ignores one of the most important facts of life: that God waits for the co-operation of man. Though often held rather vaguely and without deep conviction, it is sufficient to prevent many intelligent people from learning to pray.

For, of course, prayer has to be learned like any other of the higher human activities. It must be practised assiduously if proficiency is to be attained. It is a mistake to suppose that anybody can pray. That is only true in the sense that anybody can *begin* to pray. Anybody can learn to pray just as anybody can learn to read. But though from the very beginning our prayers may be worth-while, as from our most elementary acquaintance of the printed page exciting possibilities lie before us awaiting exploration, the more we advance in prayer the more there is to discover. The first time you touch a piano you may produce some striking chords, but it will take years of practice to make you an accomplished pianist.

If we need practice in these cultural activities, how much more do we need training in prayer, which is the highest faculty of all? It is perfectly true that any child can pray, but that does not excuse grown people praying like any child. The youth who after a term at the night school declared that he had been "all through mathematics" is not more ignorant than those who, having been taught to pray at their mothers' knees, have never advanced beyond that rudimentary stage of devotion.

When the disciples of Jesus, men who had been nurtured in the devotional wealth of the Hebrew Scriptures, came to Him with the request,[1] "Lord, teach us to pray," it was because they had learned from the example of their Master that prayer, of the kind that He practised, is a faculty that needs training. It is an exercise of the mind, an act of thought, a discipline of the emotions, an intercourse of the spirit. It is so simple that anyone can begin it; but so infinite in its possibilities that no one can ever come to an end of it.

[1] Luke xi. 1.

II

APPEARANCE AND REALITY

THERE are two aspects of life; two ways of looking at things. One we will call the material aspect, the other the spiritual.

This book, for instance, presents two aspects to anyone who is interested in it. Or we might say that this book has two parts. The first, the material part, is that which can be seen and handled, measured and weighed. The paper and the binding and the type are all material substances not without interest and value in themselves.

The other part of the book, the spiritual, is that which cannot be seen or handled, and yet it is that which gives the book most of its value. It is the message or thought which the book contains, its "contents"—what the book has to say. This we might call the real book, because it is what the book was made for. Without this the book would be a sham. It might be used as an ornament or a paperweight or a missile, but it would not be a book. Yet this real book is entirely invisible and intangible. For though we can see the type that makes the words, we cannot see or touch or measure the thought which these words express.

The thought or message of the book is entirely non-material, or, to use the word that we have already used, spiritual.

We can see that these two parts or aspects of the book, while closely related to each other, are quite distinct from each other. Concerning their relation to each, three simple but important facts become plain:

1. The material exists for the purpose of giving expression to the spiritual. The paper and type would not be here at all in the form of a book, unless there had been a thought or a meaning to express. The reason for the existence of the

material book is the previous existence of the spiritual book, and the whole purpose of the material book is to unfold or reveal or make plain the spiritual.

2. It follows that the material is created for and by the spiritual. It is the thought or message of the author which, demanding expression, has caused the book to be made.

3. The material is of temporary existence and is destructible; the spiritual is permanent and indestructible. The material book could be burned or reduced to pulp. But the thought or message of it, if it remained in the reader's mind, would not thereby be destroyed. The content of the book, though it could not be known without the book, survives its loss or destruction.

Now, what we have said of the book is true of everything, for everything has these two aspects, the material and the spiritual; the visible and the invisible; the temporal and the eternal. Just as the material book has a non-material or spiritual content that gives it its real value, so the whole material world has a significance which we must try to understand if we would know the true meaning and purpose of life.

Of this underlying meaning or significance in life we can say, as in the case of the book, that—

(1) the material world exists for the purpose of giving it expression;

(2) that it is the creator of all material things, which could never have existed without it;

(3) that it survives the existence of the material, being also pre-existent of the material.

What we have said of the whole material universe we can say also of every material thing, and in particular we can say it of the human body. It is equally true of all material things and circumstances.

(1) The body is the expression of the Spirit.
(2) The body is the creation of the Spirit.
(3) The body is survived by the Spirit.

It is easy to see, in the case of the book or the human body, that the really important part is the invisible, intangible spirit which reveals itself in the part that we can see and touch. We may call this aspect of things the spiritual, or the heavenly, or the eternal. It is the reality as distinct from the appearance. The material part is the means or medium of expression; the spiritual part is that which is expressed.

But when we consider the whole universe, what is this underlying meaning or significance of which we have spoken? What is the Spirit of which the material world is the expression?

III

PRAYER IS CONTROLLED THINKING

ALL prayer is based on the conviction that the whole visible universe is the creation and expression of an invisible Power. We might distinguish between a religious and a non-religious attitude to life by saying that the first regards the universe as the medium of a message; whereas the second believes that the message is an illusion, and that material phenomena are the only reality. The religious man sees life as a book to be read. The non-religious man admires the printing and binding, but deprecates any attempt to read it as superstition. Looking at a sunset, or the death of a hero, or the beauty of children, or the starry firmament, the religious observer declares: "There is Something in this that is speaking to me. It is a poem making its appeal to my mind and conscience." The non-religious observer says: "It is beautiful indeed, but the beauty is fortuitous and has no more message than the fancied voice that one hears in the sighing of the wind." Religion, in short, discerns a meaning in life, and a meaning implies a Person. Non-religion recognises no meaning in life, except such as phantasy may attribute to it, and therefore no Person.

Now prayer is the attempt to establish contact between man and the divine Person whose message or meaning all phenomena express. It is simply communication between man and God, or, rather, we should say between God and man, for God begins it, and man's prayers to God are always a response to God's prayer to man.

The whole of life, then, alike in Nature and history and all human experience, is God's appeal or message to man. This is not to say that everything that happens is an expression of the will and purpose of God. We shall consider later how the will of God suffers resistance by the will of man.

But this very fact that God's will can be and is obscured and hindered by man's will is also part of the divine purpose. So, while some experiences speak to us more directly of God than do others, we may say that the whole of experience is the medium of God's message to us.

Sometimes this message is called the "Word" of God. It does not consist of words, but it is what God has to say. Faith sees in the whole of life the means by which God is communicating with man. Everything has been brought into existence to express this communication or "Word". Thus the Gospel says: "In the beginning was the Word, and the Word was with God, and the Word was God. . . . All things were made by Him; and without Him was not anything made that was made."[1]

Just as the author's message brings his book into existence, so God's "Word" has brought the whole of life into existence. The material is created by the spiritual. As the Epistle says, "The things that are seen have been made out of the things that are not seen."[2]

The Christian faith lays emphasis on the truth that God, the Creator of all, is pure Spirit. He has no form or substance. "We ought not to think that God is like unto" anything.[3] While we cherish the simple and picturesque anthropomorphism of the Hebrew Scriptures, we must not think childishly of God as though He were like man. "God is spirit, and they that worship Him must worship Him in spirit and in truth."[4]

The word "Spirit" may for some readers have associations that are misleading. It may suggest something that is ghostly (in the modern sense) or the subject of occult mysteries, or something that is the preserve of particularly pious people. Perhaps it would help to clarify our thinking if we were to use the Scriptural term "Word." Word or message is something invisible and intangible. It is non-material and therefore "spiritual." Or we might say that

[1] John i. 1–13.   [2] Heb. xi. 3.   [3] Acts xvii. 29.   [4] John iv. 24.

God is Mind, or God is thought, so long as we do not use these words as exact synonyms, but only to help us understand the meaning of "Spirit."

When we say that "God is Spirit, and they that worship Him must worship in spirit,"[1] we understand that the power of God is something like the power of thought, and that worship must be an act of thought. The really important part of worship or prayer is not the words which are uttered, still less the material objects which may be used, or the posture of the body, or anything visible or tangible or audible, but the thought of the worshipping mind.

Real prayer is thinking about God; and effective prayer is right thinking about God. It may very suitably be accompanied by symbolic actions, or rapturous words, or impressive music, but the essential part of prayer is thought. It is in the realm of thought that we pray; it is there that we meet God. By "thought" we do not mean intellectual reasoning, and certainly not any kind of mental gymnastics, but just thinking as everybody thinks and as nobody can help thinking. Thought includes imagination and desire, for we cannot desire a thing without thinking of it, and it is always touched with feeling, for we can scarcely think of anything without some degree of feeling, and feelings and thoughts affect each other. We are not using "thought" in any particular psychological sense of the word, but quite simply as when someone asks, "What are you thinking about?" We are always thinking (with some degree of emotion) about something, and when we are thinking about God we are beginning to pray, and when we are thinking of God rightly we are praying aright.

It is in the realm of thought that we pray; it is there that we meet God. There is no other temple or sanctuary which does not take its sanctity from the presence within it of the thought in which God dwells.

[1] John iv. 24.

IV

THE POWER OF THOUGHT

BEFORE we proceed further let us stop to look at the astonishing power given to every human being with the ability to think.

Of all the faculties with which man is endowed there is none greater than the power of thought. For thought is the spring and source of all action, and there is no work of man which does not have its origin in his mind. The house in which we live existed first in plan—that is to say, in thought —before it took shape in physical being. Our cherished possessions were cherished as desires before we had them in substance. Great social institutions and world-wide organisations are the result of thought. Indeed, all material things, as we have already observed, have their origin in the spiritual.

But that is not all. Thought has another and more immediate effect on our lives than is usually observed. Not only do physical objects exist first in thought, but our material circumstances take their character from our thoughts. It is not true, of course, that we can conjure up material objects merely by thinking of them. But our thoughts "colour" our circumstances, in the sense that if our thoughts are sad and gloomy our circumstances tend to be so too. If our thoughts are cheerful and happy, our circumstances are likely to be so also. If we think morbidly of suffering, we shall experience suffering. If we contemplate violence, violence will make its way into our experience. We invariably bring into our circumstances what we take into our thoughts.

This is not to say that the moment we think of any event that event will take place. That is quite evidently untrue. Happily, the thought of illness or accident or other evil can pass through our minds without our experiencing any such thing. By a merciful Providence, thoughts do not immediately take shape in material conditions. There are, moreover, other factors in the making of our circumstances than our own thoughts. The thoughts of our neighbours, for instance, and of the whole community in which we live, contribute to the making of our environment. But whatever we think of habitually will certainly tend to reproduce itself in our circumstances. If a man continually thinks in terms of want and poverty, he will have a strong tendency to become or remain poor, even while making efforts to get rich. If he allows his thoughts to dwell habitually on sickness and disease, he is likely sooner or later to experience ill health, either in his own person or in his immediate neighbours or in both. If he broods over the wickedness of humanity he will soon find abundant evidence of it in his own life. If he is haunted by fear of accident and injury, these will very probably overtake him.

Precautions and restraints may have the effect of postponing or modifying the effect of thinking upon experience, though some psychologists would claim that attempts to evade the natural law by which thoughts take shape in material circumstances only accelerate the process which they try to stop. Instances of such futile attempts would be found in frantic efforts to make peace while the whole world is thinking in terms of war, or in measures taken to restore to health a patient whom everybody is expecting to die.

While it is true that our thoughts help to create our circumstances, it is also true, of course, that our circumstances give rise to our thoughts. That is to say, thinking and experience interact. We might describe life as a struggle between thought and circumstance, in which either our thoughts get the better of our circumstances, or our circumstances get the better of our thoughts. Certain it is that if we do not master our environment our environment will master us.

If we begin to think ourselves ill used we shall soon create a situation in which we are ill used, and that fact will intensify our thoughts of self-pity which in turn will add to the causes of our self-pity. We are here in a vicious circle of thought and its projection on life, from the grip of which we can only break loose by steady and sustained meditation on the goodness of God. That will soon take effect in happier circumstances which will help us to happier thoughts, which again will make life happier still.

Our thoughts not only help to make our circumstances, they also determine our character. If we think of doing wrong, whether from secret desire or from wholesome fear, we shall be inclined to do it. Perhaps we seldom, if ever, do evil unless and until we have accepted the evil in our thoughts. We give in to a temptation in our hearts before we succumb to it in action. We sin in thought before we sin in deed. On the other hand, the only real righteousness is that which is "by faith" taken into our thoughts in contemplation and desire. When we delight in goodness then we are really good and not otherwise.

It would be inaccurate to speak of our thought as the main dynamic in life. It is the divine Spirit which alone is creative and dynamic. But by our thoughts we admit into our lives, or exclude from them, the divine power. By our thoughts (if we may use such a mechanical metaphor) we gear into the thought of God. In meditation on the being and work of God we put His power into effective operation, alike in our circumstances and our characters.

It will be noticed that we are using the word "thought," not in its sense of intellectual reasoning, but in the simple and popular sense of what passes through our minds. This "stream of consciousness," which never ceases to flow during our waking hours, is of the utmost importance for our well-being and that of our neighbours, though its importance is often overlooked. We are always *thinking* of something in the sense of allowing it to occupy our minds. It is that content of the mind that makes or mars our lives.

Thought in this sense includes emotion, for there is always some degree of emotion aroused by what we are thinking of. Some objects of thought make us angry, others make us sorry, and others give us pleasure. The emotional quality of our thought is an important factor in its power to determine our circumstances and to mould our characters.

It is our thoughts that make us what we are. "As a man thinketh in his heart so is he."[1] Our thoughts are expressed on our faces both momentarily and permanently. But not only our facial appearance (and to a large extent our carriage and demeanour) but our character or personality is made by our thinking. A man who thinks himself inferior will gradually take on a corresponding attitude to life. One who thinks proudly will tend to walk proudly. A haunting fear, a sense of humour, self-importance and a quick human sympathy are all written on the face and figure and can usually be easily recognised.

Think of good and you will be good. Fill your mind with love and joy and courage and sincerity and diligence and self-control and all the other good qualities of character, and they will undoubtedly find expression in your own nature. Contemplate virtue and you are likely to be virtuous.

Well does the ancient wisdom of the Book of Proverbs say:

> *"Keep thy thoughts with all diligence*
> *For out of them are the issues of life."*[2]

[1] Prov. xxiii. 7.   [2] Prov. iv. 23.

V

READJUSTMENT TO LIFE

THE suggestion has been made that it might help us to understand the truth that "God is Spirit" if we paraphrased it, "God is Thought." The being of God is far beyond our comprehension, but it may help us to begin to think rightly about God if we remember that thought is creative, and that God, the Creator, is Thought. This is not all that we can say about the divine nature, but it is one truth that can help us to understand what we mean when we speak of "God."

Now, if Thought is the creator, that means that everything that exists has been brought into being and is sustained in being by God's thought. "In Him we live and move and have our being."[1] We are ourselves, together with all the material objects around us, and with the whole universe of Nature, dependent on the divine thought. It is thought, and nothing else, that is creative. This is what the Gospel means when it says of the *Logos*, "All things were made by it, and without it nothing was made that was made."[2] Thought is the creator, and the creative power is thought.

But if everything owes its origin to God's thought, how do we account for all the evil in life? Are disease and want and war and ignorance and sin created by God? This is the problem of evil, and though we cannot hope to solve in a few words one of the chief problems of philosophy, perhaps, even at the risk of over-simplifying what is very complex and profound, we can try to understand it like this:

God's thought is perfect—absolutely holy and pure and good, and everything made by the divine thought is quite heavenly.

[1] Acts xvii. 28.   [2] John i. 3.

But God created the world to be the home of man, and He made man to be akin to Himself in spirit, so that communion or fellowship between God and man might be possible. That is what is meant by saying that "God created man in His own image."[1] Spirit, of course, has no image, being immaterial, having no form or substance. But here the word is used in its meaning of "likeness." God created man to be like Himself, of the same kind. That means that God, being Thought, made man also capable of thought.

But when God gave man ability to think there arose the danger that human thought would differ from the divine thought. For thought is free, and man, being made in the likeness of his creator, was enabled to exercise a similar, if limited, creative faculty. Now, this is exactly what has happened. Man's thought has marred the work of God's thought. What was created in perfection by the divine thought has been distorted and defiled by the human thought, with the result that the life that God made perfect and heavenly has been invaded by all sorts of evil.

But if wrong thinking is the cause of all the evil in life, right thinking is the cause of all the good. If we could only bring our minds into harmony with the divine mind; if our thoughts could reflect the thoughts of God, then life would assume the character which God meant it to have. If the human mind could be brought into agreement with the divine mind, then life would be immediately transformed in accordance with God's will.

The Good News of the Christian faith is that this *can* be done, and it calls on us to do it. "Change your minds" was the message of our Lord when He came preaching into Galilee, "the realm of Heaven is at hand! Repent and believe the gospel."[2] Repentance means a change in our way of thinking, and our Lord's call to a change of mentality

[1] Gen. i. 27. [2] Matt. iv. 17; Mark i. 15

(metanoia) suggests that if we think aright, if we take a right view of things, and a right attitude to life, we shall thereby let heaven into our lives, the heaven which is not far off, but close at hand ready to pervade our world, as the light is ready to stream in the moment the curtains are drawn. This recalls the words of the Epistle, "Be not conformed to this world, but be ye transformed by the renewing of your minds, that ye may prove what is that good and acceptable and perfect will of God."[1] Or as the prophet said:

> *"Let the wicked forsake his way,*
> *And the unrighteous man his thoughts:*
> *And let him return unto the Lord,*
> *And he will have mercy upon him;*
> *And to our God,*
> *For he will abundantly pardon."*[2]

Righteousness is essentially and originally righteousness of thought, and therefore when we return to God in thought we return to Him indeed.

To abolish the evil in the world, we must abolish the wrong thinking, the perverted mind, the fears, the phantasies, the resentments, in a word the "sin," that is the cause of the evil. Sin is opposition to God; it is the departure of our minds from the mind of God, the deflection of human will from the divine will. To destroy sin, and rid the world of its baneful consequences, we must destroy the discrepancy between human thought and divine thought. Our minds must be brought into harmony with God's mind. Or, in other words, we must reconcile man to God.

This is just what the gospel declares to be possible. This is the very thing that Christ has done. "God in Christ was reconciling the world unto Himself."[3] The Christian

---

[1] Rom. xii. 2. [2] Isa. lv. 7. [3] 2 Cor. v. 19.

message is one of reconciliation to God. Sometimes the word for reconciliation (*katallage*) is translated "at-one-ment" or agreement.[1] It means a complete change toward someone. It is the restoring of our minds to perfect harmony with the mind of God.

Perhaps in passing we ought to notice that in Christian theology reconciliation always means the reconciling of man to God and not of God to man. The idea that God needs to be placated by sacrifice is sub-Christian. Strangely enough, God *is* reconciled to man, in the sense of regarding him with absolute love. It is man that needs to be reconciled to the goodness and wisdom of God. It is the stupid and rebellious children who need to be reconciled to their Father. Our salvation consists in being reconciled to God and to the life that God appoints for us. That does not mean that we are reconciled to the world as it is. Far from it! But in Christ we are reconciled to life as God made it and as God wants it to be.

To be reconciled to God does not mean merely that we are thinking about God, but that we are beginning to think as God thinks, that what is in our minds is akin to the divine Mind. It means that we share something of the purpose and will of God. "Let this mind be in you that was also in Christ."[2]

When we have the right mentality, when our thoughts are in harmony with the divine Thought, then the power of God works freely in us and in our circumstances. Of course, the power of God is always working in us, or we should not be living at all, but we can and do obstruct and hinder God's loving thought of us by our wrong and ignorant thoughts of Him. What we must realise is that our thoughts have the effect either of hindering or helping God's care of us and of our neighbours. As often as, and to the degree in which, we bring our thoughts into agreement with God's heavenly thought, spiritual power comes

[1] Rom. v. 11.   [2] Phil. ii. 5.

flooding into our lives destroying evil and creating good.¹

We are not concerned here with the question *how* we are reconciled to God, but with the fact that we can be and that the consequence of being so reconciled is th transformation of our lives. Call it "redemption" or "salvation" or "ransom" or use any other word you can think of that means a complete change from evil to good. This is what happens when we "change our mentality and believe." Evil as the world is, it can be redeemed, and the process of redemption begins in and through us as soon as we turn in thought and desire to God.

It is not we who redeem the world, but God. All we have to do is to allow God's power to work in our lives. And we do so when we bring our thoughts into harmony with God's thoughts. When we receive God into our minds, we take Him into our lives.

¹ Cf. this passage from a devotional classic: "As soon as a man turneth himself in spirit, and with his whole heart and mind entereth into the mind of God which is above time, all that ever he hath lost is restored in a moment. And if a man were to do thus a thousand times in a day, each time a fresh and real union would take place; and in this sweet and divine work standeth the truest and fullest union that may be in this present time. For he who hath attained thereto asketh nothing further, for he hath found the Kingdom of Heaven and Eternal Life on earth" (*Theologia Germanica*).

VI

HOW TO PRAY

PRAYER is the activity of thought by which we admit God into our lives. A wrong emphasis is put on prayer when we regard it as asking God for gifts. This emphasis is suggested in the very word "prayer," which means the humble and earnest request for favours. Asking is indeed one essential part of prayer, for what we are not asking for we do not want and, as we shall observe more carefully later,[1] spiritual gifts cannot be given where they are not wanted. The asking need not, and must not, be formal. It is an attitude of mind which, though it may be expressed in formal petition, is more truly and effectively expressed in our willingness to receive.

Prayer, in fact, is not so much asking as receiving. As sincere asking is willingness to receive, we need not put these two aspects of prayer in contrast. But we must not put undue emphasis on asking, as though we were more eager to obtain than God to give. The contrary is true. God offers His gifts to us far more earnestly than we desire to have them.

We do not need to beseech or implore God to be good or merciful, for it is His very nature to be so. We do not need to beg for the things which He, in His divine humility, is begging us to receive. Instead of calling upon God to give, we should do better to call upon ourselves to take. "Your Father knoweth what things ye have need of before ye ask Him."[2]

A large part of prayer, then, must be receiving. Here the question arises: How do we receive? The answer is very simple. It is: By taking God and His gifts into our minds

[1] P. 44. [2] Matt. vi. 8.

and dwelling upon them in our thoughts. For what we take into our thoughts we take into our lives.

This means that prayer must be largely meditation. It is thinking of God. Prayer that is centred on ourselves and our needs and our sufferings, or even on our sins, is of poor value. We certainly must confess our sins, but in such a way as to cast them from us, to separate ourselves from them, to have them destroyed by God's forgiveness. In true prayer we forget ourselves and concentrate on God and His goodness, His love, His righteousness. What God has to say to us is more important than what we have to say to God.

We begin then with the thought of God. Of course we cannot think of God as we ought, or as He really is. Our minds cannot comprehend the infinite greatness of God who dwelleth "in light inaccessible."[1] But we must try to form the best conception of God that we can, and the more we try the better we shall succeed. Our thoughts will gradually become purified of gross and childish ideas, and we shall be able to think of God more and more worthily.

Remember what has already been said of God as Spirit. We must not make any mental image of Him, "or any likeness of anything."[2] There is nothing material about God. He is not to be confused with His creation, and we must not worship the creature rather than the Creator. He can be seen only in His manifestations, but He is not to be identified with the manifestation, any more than the artist is with his picture.

Let us begin by thinking of God as Love. We all have some experience of human love and kindness in which the divine Love is revealed. Try to think of God, then, as perfect love, a self-giving and self-revealing love. Think of the gentleness and patience and humility of love, and remember that love is also the supreme power in life. Think of love as expressed in forgiveness. Read some passages of Scripture such as 1 Cor. xiii or 1 John iv which describe

[1] 1 Tim. vi. 15.   [2] Exod. xx. 4.

love. Then dwell on the thought that God is love, and that love is God.

From this we can pass to the thought of God as righteousness, for the only real righteousness is love. Love alone is the fulfilling of the moral law. We all know good men and women in whose presence we have been at once humbled and helped. These imperfect instances of righteousness may lead us to the thought of the perfect Righteousness. Despite all the wickedness of the world, righteousness is at work, and will prevail.

Perfect love is also perfect wisdom, so let us think of the wisdom of God as revealed in Nature and History and Providence. Think of the wonderful discoveries of science, or the faculties of the human mind, or look up into the heavens, where "the firmament sheweth his handiwork,"[1] and then remember that all that is but part of the "loving wisdom of our God." All knowledge is His, and all learning, who sees the end from the beginning, Who is the Universal Mind, the Father of our spirits.

From this we pass easily to the conception of God as the Holy Spirit of Truth, who will guide us into all truth.[2] This is that indwelling Spirit "whom the world cannot receive because it seeth Him not, neither knoweth Him, but ye know Him, for He dwelleth with you and shall be in you."[3] Truth is akin to love, or we might say it is one aspect of love. Both are names for God. Truth, like love, shows us life as it really is, and delivers us from fears and errors, phantasies and illusions. Superstition and fear can hold us in cruel bondage, but "the truth shall make you free."[4]

But by far the best way to think of God is to see Him as He is revealed in Jesus. There was a Man in whose presence His contemporaries felt that God was with them. Within a generation after His death it was possible for one to write, "in Him dwelleth all the fulness of the Godhead bodily."[5]

[1] Ps. xix. 1. [2] John xvi. 13. [3] John xiv. 17.
[4] John viii. 32. [5] Col. ii. 9.

We should not, however, think of Jesus as God, but think of God as revealed in Jesus. We must not attempt to confine the divine in the human, but see the human as possessed by the divine. All the time we are thinking in terms of the Spirit and not of the body. "Even though we have known Christ after the flesh, yet now henceforth know we Him so no more."[1] This is important. Meditation should not be content to dwell on scenes in the life of our Lord, or on imagination of His bodily appearance, but should cherish the spiritual qualities which the record of His life and death reveals.

We should think of all the characteristics of our Lord, all that goes to make Him what He is. Think, for instance, of His joy; His very gaiety of spirit gave offence to some good but severe people. Or think of His courage, of His calm serenity of faith, of His kindness, His gentleness, His humility, His sincerity, His capacity for friendship, and for forgiveness. Remember that God is like that. The supreme Power in life is of the same character as Jesus. Life itself will unfold to the adventurous spirit the same qualities that are displayed in Him. That is what we mean when we say that He is the Son of God, that He and the Father of all are of kindred spirit, and that He is the Lord of all life.

We cannot, of course, think of all that we know of God every time we pray. But we should always begin by lifting up our thoughts in accordance with the ancient bidding:

> *"Lift up your thoughts.*
> *We lift them up unto the Lord."*

In other words, prayer should begin, after the example of our Lord's Prayer, with adoration. We begin in this way, not as is sometimes supposed, out of compliment to God! But because we cannot rightly engage in prayer at all until

---

[1] 2 Cor. v. 16.

we have formed in our minds the highest conception of God that we can. Prayer begins with the thought of God and not of anything else, least of all ourselves. We will come to ourselves presently. But we must begin with God and with the highest thought of God that we can reach.

VII

IS TROUBLE SENT BY GOD?

WHILE life in this world is rightly regarded as a discipline or school of character, there are many troubles which beset us which are no part of the will of God. The life of faith is not a heroic endurance of evil; it is the victory which overcometh the world. We must not pretend that we are overcoming that to which we are in fact submitting.

Too often a Stoic fortitude is made a substitute for the triumphant Christian life. Submission is not a Christian virtue, unless it is submission to the will of God. But that is submission to what is supremely good, and "submission" seems hardly the right word for the acceptance of that which exceeds "all that we can ask or think" in blessedness. We ought rather to speak of *rising* to the will of God, or *achieving* His purpose for us, always remembering that we cannot rise to it by our own effort, but only by God working within us "to will and to do of His good pleasure."[1]

We must consider, therefore, whether many of the troubles to which we are subject are really ordained of God, or, on the contrary, are imposed upon us by our own misconception of God's will, by our fears and suspicions and resentments. We shall find that many of the pains and distresses and disabilities from which we suffer are imposed upon us, not by God, but by ourselves. Our sufferings are the creation, not of God's thought, but of man's, and not only of the thought of mankind at large, but the result of our own mentality.

Sometimes when this is observed it is resented as a reflection on the character of the sufferer, but there is no more

[1] Phil. ii. 13.

IS TROUBLE SENT BY GOD? 33

ground of offence than in the case of a patient who is told that his pains are due to unsuitable food, and who cheerfully submits to drastic changes in his diet. Surely no greater reproach is involved in saying to a sufferer, "Your mental diet is harmful; we prescribe a change in your food for thought."

The truth is that our condition and our circumstances are alike influenced by our thoughts. We are told that the truth is not palatable, but a truth which contains such a simple remedy for so much suffering should be received with rejoicing, as indeed it was received with joy and triumph by the first disciples of Christ. The Acts of the Apostles is the record of the free and victorious life of the early Church, whose message was the same as that of our Lord Himself in Galilee, Repent, change your mentality!

This is the truth that makes us free. Emancipation lies in the realisation that it is not God's will that life in this world of His should be a "vale of tears" filled with sorrow and trouble. That there is a precious element of redemptive and vicarious suffering in life is not denied. We shall return to that later. But all suffering is not redemptive, and much of it is useless. What is contended here is that there is a vast amount of unnecessary and quite unredemptive suffering, which, so far from helping the work of God, only hinders and opposes it. Aches and pains, want and privation, accidents and calamities, all manner of limitations and inhibitions, domestic dissension, industrial strife, far from being the will of God and appointed by Him, are in direct contradiction to His will and flagrant disregard of it. As the Epistle says, "God hath not appointed us to wrath, but to obtain salvation."[1]

But what is God's will? While we must not pretend that the will of the Almighty is completely known by our finite minds, we must equally beware of the agnosticism that disclaims all knowledge of the divine mind. God has

[1] 1 Thess. v. 9.

not left Himself without a witness, and He has declared His nature and will very plainly in Christ.[1]

We know, for instance, that it is God's will to extend to us the loving care of His providence, and that we ought not to be anxious about the material things which God knows we need. We know that it is the will of God to forgive, and that we should forgive each other instead of cherishing resentful or vindictive feelings. We know that it is God's will in Christ to heal diseases. We know that it is God's will that we should not succumb to our moral weaknesses, but grow towards perfection of character. We know that we are destined by the will of God to become His children, partaking of His divine nature.[2]

With this knowledge before us, we must examine our experience to ascertain whether our sufferings are such as are imposed by God or only by ourselves. Many people believe that their troubles are sent to them for their good, and that the right attitude towards them is that of patient endurance. Sometimes troubles are taken to be "the chastening of the Lord,"[3] whether as direct punishment for sin, or part of a general discipline that makes for strength and purity of character. The question arises, Does God use evil to punish us? Or we might put it thus: Does God do evil for our good?

[1] Rom. i. 19–20. [2] 2 Pet. i. 4. [3] Heb. xii. 5 ff.

VIII

DOES GOD PUNISH US?

THIS question can only be answered here very briefly with a blunt negative. God does not punish in the usual sense of that word. Men believe that the best way of dealing with wrongdoing is to punish the wrongdoer by making him suffer, and when men do wrong they expect to be so punished. But God has another way of dealing with wrongdoing; He forgives it. Instead of the wrongdoer suffering, the one he has wronged suffers. This is the principle of vicarious suffering, "the just for the unjust."[1] It is redemptive suffering, the only kind of suffering that is appointed by God.

The essence of the Christian gospel is just this, that sin, with all its evil consequences, can be abolished, and is abolished by forgiveness. Our Lord used the metaphor of debt, and said that just as a debt is cancelled by a word, so that it no longer exists, so sin is put out of existence by forgiveness.

For those whose minds have been soaked in the thought that suffering is the punishment demanded by the moral order, the principle of forgiveness is so hard to understand that even those who are assured of their forgiveness in Christ have often supposed that forgiveness to be made possible by the punishment of Christ on their behalf. This penal view of the Cross is not in accordance with the teaching of our Lord Himself, and has done much mischief. We cannot enter into a discussion of it here, but it may be observed that even on this view God does not punish man for his sin. The explanation of this fact has sometimes been erroneous, but the fact itself has been acknowledged in all sound

[1] I Pet. iii.

evangelical doctrine, that there is now no punishment for sin.

It is sometimes said, "Of course God forgives sin, but only on condition of our repentance, and to bring us to repentance He must punish us." This statement contains two fallacies. (1) Repentance is not a prior condition of forgiveness. God does not withhold His forgiveness until the sinner repents. "While we were yet sinners Christ died for us."[1] It is not repentance that produces forgiveness, but forgiveness that produces repentance. "Or despisest thou the riches of His goodness, and forbearance and longsuffering, not knowing that the goodness [*chrestos*] of God leadeth thee to repentance."[2] (2) Punishment never does produce true repentance. Only forgiveness can do that. The wrongdoer who is punished is made sorry for himself, but not for his sin. Or sometimes he is made rather proud of himself as a martyr and hero, and therefore proud of his sin. But only in unusual circumstances is a culprit brought to repentance by punishment. Having been moved to repentance by other means, he may assent to the punishment as the due reward of his sins. But unless there are other factors in the case making for repentance, punishment usually has the effect of making the sinner only wish he had sinned more. Punishment makes men wary of detection, but not of sin.

While man is concerned to bring the sinner to "justice" and to make the punishment fit the crime, the way of God is quite different. He has not dealt with us after our sins, or rewarded us according to our iniquities."[3] "If Thou, Lord, shouldest mark iniquity, O Lord, who should stand? Yet there is forgiveness with Thee, that Thou mayest be worshipped."[4] God in Christ was reconciling the world unto Himself, not imputing their trespasses unto them."[5] The ancient Hebrew writers already begin to perceive the

[1] Rom. v. 8.   [2] Rom. ii. 4.   [3] Ps. ciii. 10.
[4] Ps. cxxx. 3-4.   [5] 2 Cor. v. 19.

truth that God does not punish the sinner, but this astonishing fact is set forth plainly in the New Testament. We are saved by an act, not of justice, but of forgiveness. In Christ we have "redemption, even the forgiveness of sins."[1]

But does not God punish men for the sins that He forgives? While forgiving the sin, does He not nevertheless punish the sinner for his good? The answer to this question must be that whether it is for the sinner's good or not, even God cannot punish sins and forgive them at the same time. If you punish the sinner, you do not forgive him; and if you forgive him, you do not punish him. You cannot both collect a debt and cancel it; and you cannot exact reparation and at the same time forgive. Forgiveness means that the wronged person takes upon himself the cost and suffering consequent upon the sin, and he does this on behalf of and instead of the sinner, whose sorrow and suffering and even reparations can never make up for the wrong he has done. Forgiveness lays the suffering, not on the forgiven person, but on the forgiver. It is the only practicable and wise, as it is the only really right and the divine way of dealing with sin.

Well, then, may not much of our suffering be vicarious, and ought not we to accept it as part of the redemptive suffering by which evil is overcome? We will try to answer this question in a later chapter, for it is so important that it calls for special consideration. There certainly is a kind of suffering which has redemptive value and which we ought never to try to escape. It is the suffering of the Cross—that is, the persecution which we bear as a result of our attack upon evil and our witness to the right. Here we are speaking of suffering of a very different kind, of useless, unnecessary suffering which does no good to anybody, and the relief of which would be a blessing to all.

[1] Col. i. 14, Eph. i. 7.

IX

DO WE GET OUR DESERTS?

THERE is indeed a principle in life whereby wrongdoing eventually leads to disaster. God is Love, and He has made His universe in such a way that it can serve no other purpose than that of love. Every form of evil therefore must ultimately defeat itself.

But it is not true that the individual wrongdoer invariably suffers for the wrong he does. No one can sin without suffering spiritually, which just amounts to saying that no one sins without sinning. For sin is its own severest penalty. But to say that sin is its own punishment is to use the word "punishment" in a derived sense. If the magistrate should say to the delinquent, "Your own evil conduct is a far more severe penalty than any I can impose. I will therefore impose none," he does not thereby punish the offender. On the contrary, he dispenses with punishment.

While the sinner always suffers spiritually (for sin is spiritual infirmity), he does not always suffer materially. Indeed, the unscrupulous person often avoids suffering which a more conscientious person would incur. In the present state of society iniquity is frequently rewarded by honours and wealth. Selfishness is often successful in the enjoyment of comforts which the good neighbour must forgo. As the Psalmist observed, "Lo, these are the ungodly that prosper!"[1] So far from the wicked invariably meeting the punishment they deserve, they frequently escape it.

We live in an ordered world, and if we defy the laws of Nature, which are the laws of God, we must abide the consequences. If we neglect the laws of health, we fall victims to disease. If we ignore the law of gravitation, it will not be suspended in our favour. But it is one thing to allow those

[1] Ps. lxxiii. 12.

who defy Nature to take the consequences, and another to impose penalties upon them. God does not save us from all the natural consequences of our folly, but neither does He impose suffering as a penalty for being foolish.

It is clear that we are not living in a world in which we get our deserts. Justice is an attribute of God in the sense of making men just, but not in the sense of apportioning rewards and punishments. God is not concerned to give us our deserts in the due reward of our sins. His purpose is one of goodness and mercy far exceeding our merits. Life does not yield us what we ought to receive, or what we have any just claim to, but it pours out upon us, if we are willing to accept them, gifts far beyond our deserts and even our desires.

We must not then suppose that our troubles are laid upon us by God as penalties. Many of them, at least, are imposed upon us by ourselves. "Let no man when he is tried say, I am being tested by God, for God has nothing to do with evil nor does He try any man. . . . Every gift is good and every faculty is perfect as it comes down from the Creator of the heavenly bodies in Whom there is no variation or eclipse."[1] The fact is that God is absolute good, and His will for us is invariably good. It is our deflection from His heavenly will that causes the evils or "trials" from which we suffer.

How we cling to the belief that evil somehow does us good! God indeed can and does bring good out of evil, but He can and does bring far more good out of good. God blesses and helps us not by means of evil but in spite of evil. Evil can never contribute to good. Our sin does not help us to be righteous; we can only become righteous by forsaking our sin. So evil can never minister to good except by disappearing and ceasing to exist.

Life is good—essentially and originally good. It is the means through which a good God is expressing His love for

[1] Jas. i. 13-17.

us. Life as God made it has been spoilt and fouled by the deflection of the human mind from the divine Mind, that is to say, by sin. But from sin we can be saved, and that means that life can be restored to its heavenly or eternal quality.

This is the meaning of "salvation." We are saved or rescued, not from the consequences of sin in some other life, but from sin and its consequences in this life. Christian faith is, of course, an assurance concerning the life to come, but the life to come begins in this present life. The eternal or heavenly life begins here. And it is a life in which evil has no rightful place, and is no more to be tolerated than sin itself. Our salvation in Christ is complete. In Him we are restored to a right relation to God. We are given the power as we are given the right to become the children of God, and "if children then heirs, heirs of God and joint heirs with Christ."[1]

We may be quite sure, then, that evil, in whatever form, is not sent by God. When we say that God is good, we do not mean that He is "good for us," as we might suppose some unpleasant medicine to be. We mean that God Himself in His very being is absolute goodness. There can no more be evil in God than there can be darkness in light. God's will is always "good, acceptable, and perfect."[2]

If we are to do the will of God, or, rather, if God's will is to be done in us, we must relinquish our hold upon evil. When we do that evil will relinquish its hold upon us. Let it go. Realise that it is not the will of God. As the prodigal did in the far country, let us come to ourselves and lay hold upon the truth that the abundant and infinite goodness of God awaits us if only we make up our minds to arise and leave behind us the suffering and penury into which we have fallen.

Let us pray then for release from every kind of evil in the sure confidence that in so doing we are asking for God's will to be done in us.

[1] Rom. viii. 17.   [2] Rom. xii. 2.

X
PRAYING FOR HEALTH

CONSIDER, first, one of the commonest evils by which we are afflicted—sickness and disease. This is not the only manifestation of evil from which we may seek relief in the prayer of faith, but there are special reasons for believing that disease is never the will of God for any of His creatures, and that therefore prayers for healing are most acceptable to Him.

The teaching of the New Testament, and the experience of the early Church, seem to be quite clear and emphatic. The healing ministry of our Lord occupies a very important place in the Gospel history. To ignore it, or to minimise its significance, is to obscure an aspect of the Christian message which the evangelists must have considered essential. Take away the "miracles" from either the Gospels or the Acts and not only is a very large part of these Scriptures lost, but the sequence and significance of the narrative is spoilt. Instance follows instance of the exercise of healing power by Jesus, until the impression is given that healing of disease is one of the chief credentials of Messiahship. We are repeatedly told, not only that our Lord healed large numbers of sick and infirm people who were brought to Him, but also that He imparted to His disciples power and authority to heal in His name.[1] In the Acts of the Apostles the healing of infirmity takes almost an equal place with the declaration of the Resurrection, and indeed is regarded as a witness and proof of the power of the risen Saviour.[2]

If, then, we see in Jesus the perfect revelation of God, we cannot doubt that it is the nature and will of God to heal

---

[1] Mark i. 32–4, vi. 7; Matt. iv. 23–4, ix. 35, x. 1, xiv. 35–0; Luke iv. 40, vi. 17–19, ix. 1–2.

[2] Acts iii. 15–16, iv. 9–10, 29–30.

disease as it is to forgive sin. God permits disease, as He permits sin, but both are contrary to His will, and both are expelled as the will of God is admitted. We have not fully entered into our heritage in the gospel until we realise that Christ is the Saviour alike from infirmity and disease as from sin.

That disease is not the will of God we recognise every time we call in the doctor or seek the help of medical science in hospital or clinic. Any sane and wholesome view of life must regard illness as something to be got rid of. An invalid who remained ill through neglect of a proved remedy, cherishing his infirmity rather than seeking health would receive little sympathy. A healthy mind seeks a healthy body. Every good man must wish to be fit and well. To prefer invalidism would be a sign of depravity.

Nevertheless, the belief that disease can be and ought to be healed by prayer is vigorously and sometimes indignantly resisted. The objection is not to healing, but to faith healing. People who cheerfully submit to painful and hazardous treatment in hospital cannot believe that God will heal them in any other way. Like Naaman, they take offence at the very simplicity of faith. They believe in healing, but only by material means. They expect God to heal them, but only in ways of man's own choosing. And if these should fail they will endure ill health with all its painful disabilities for the rest of their lives rather than seek healing by any other means.

There is no lack of faith, but faith has been transferred from spiritual to material forces. No doubt we are all much influenced by the materialism of the age in which we live. Natural science has, during the last century, transformed human life by its far-reaching discoveries. For its marvellous achievements, we may well give thanks and honour to the devoted savants and scientists who, by faithful and self-sacrificing research, have unfolded the secrets of Nature. That the knowledge we have gained has often been put to base uses, or withheld by avarice from the free enjoyment by all, is not the fault of science, but of the vulgarity that has abused its benefits.

But the rapid advance of material science has had one result which often escapes notice, and the effect of which, even when observed, is not always fully appreciated. It has tended to shift belief from the unseen powers which underlie phenomena to the phenomena themselves, and a strong suggestion has been made to the modern mind that a study of the superficial facts and appearances exhausts the possibilities of knowledge. This phase of materialism is doubtless temporary, and a proper mental balance will be recovered by later generations. But just in this century, while we have gained so much valuable knowledge about material things, we have lost thereby for the time being much of our even more precious knowledge of things spiritual.

We of this age have grown up in a world in which natural science has been doing miracles and, naturally, we are deeply impressed by the power of material forces and the apparent sequence of cause and effect. We realise that we live in an ordered universe, and that the divine power is manifested in the operation of natural law. Expectation of "miracles" is rightly denounced as ignorant dependence on the fortuitous and fanciful which refuses to face up to the facts of life, and to undergo the wholesome discipline of law and order. It is not in the freakish or eccentric that we look for signs of God, but rather in the normal course of His providence.

All this is true and therefore a gain to true religion. The danger, however, of living in an age in which material science has achieved such astounding triumphs and made even more astounding claims, is that we become so absorbed in the material part of life, that we lose sight of the spiritual part which alone gives it significance. This spiritual sphere, of which we have already said that it is the true home of man, has also its laws which invariably operate according to the will of the Creator. The Unseen and Eternal is also part of God's ordered universe, and when we fulfil the conditions upon which spiritual laws operate they also become effective in our lives.

The law of life which Jesus discovered and proclaimed is that "acording to your faith it shall be done unto you."[1] Life will be in accordance with our expectations. Our circumstances correspond to our thoughts. This is a law of Nature the operation of which is invariable. What you take into your mind in meditation, you take into your life as fact. This law is universal; it works for the scoundrel as well as for the saint, and for the unlettered as well as for the intellectual. It is not claimed, of course, that this is the only law which affects our circumstances. The operation of this law, like that of other laws of Nature, may be and usually is modified by other factors, but the law itself never fails to work, though its results may vary in different cases. The fact that a balloon rises does not disprove the law of gravity, but rather confirms it.

When we pray for health and healing we are appealing to the laws of God's ordered universe. God Himself is absolute good. The evil in life (of which disease is one manifestation) is no part of His perfect will, but is rather the result of our departure from His will. In other words, it is due to our sin. But when we return to God in thought and desire, when we are restored to agreement and harmony with His mind, then His will can be accomplished in our lives.

God's will being a will of righteousness, and of truth and of love, cannot compel us to obedience, or force itself upon us. God, being of the nature of truth and beauty and goodness, never imposes His will, but appeals to us in all gentleness and humility. Prayer is the act of thought by which we consent to God's will and admit it into our lives. It cannot come without admission, but it is never admitted without entering in power.

[1] Matt. ix. 29.

This is not the rejection of law in favour of freakish exception; it is the fulfilment of the conditions necessary for the operation of a law which is inherent in life. When we thus put the law of faith into operation, we are denying the disorder of evil, and asserting the perfect order of God's will.

When we receive God's will of health (which is just order, as contrasted with disorder) into our lives, no "miracle" happens. God's providence is indeed "miraculous" in the sense that it is wonderful. Our feeble faith is often taken by surprise—surprise that so little faith should accomplish so much. It is miraculous in the sense that love is miraculous, or that genius is. It is miraculous in the sense that it is "supernatural," belonging to an order of life that is beyond natural science, but there are no miracles in the spiritual life if by miracle is understood the breaking of law and the setting aside of God's order.

When we pray for healing, we are not demanding "intervention" on the part of divine power to disrupt the ordered life which God has made our home. We are asking for God's known will in Christ to be done.

XI

REASONS FOR "UNANSWERED PRAYER"

PERHAPS the chief reason (we shall discuss some of the others later) why people who do believe in prayer and practise it regularly nevertheless do not pray for healing is that in their experience this sort of prayer is unavailing. If they were convinced that invalids and cripples could be restored to health in response to prayer they would make no further objection to prayer for healing. But the evidence of the facts seems to them plainly to deny that God heals disease unless by means of medical science. Of course, there are cases in which the patient is not really ill, but only imagines himself to be so. Such cases it is agreed may be amenable to prayer. But in the case of real organic diseases, if they pray for recovery from them at all, it is only to ask the divine blessing upon the medical and surgical treatment in which they do have faith. The plain fact is, such people would say, prayer does not heal, and there is no use pretending that it does. Christian Science and Lourdes may produce a few sensational cures among hysterical patients, but these are not the normal experience of ordinary sane humanity.

There are many others who would like to believe that disease is subject to prayer, but who, though they have heard of instances of faith healing and of persons who are endowed with unusual healing powers, have never found their own prayers to have the effect of removing even slight disorders, for the relief of which in themselves and others they have been driven to the usual popular remedies. Believing that our Lord did heal disease, and that He taught His disciples to do so, they wonder why the Church to-day has no power of this kind. But the fact appears to be that it has not, unless the beneficent work of our hospitals is the continuation and counterpart of Christ's healing ministry, as our prayers on Hospital Sunday take for granted. The conclusion seems to be that, despite the New Testament, we must not expect to be healed by spiritual means to-day. In some cases, of course—perhaps in a very large number—prayer and other spiritual helps may, by raising the spirits of the patient, assist the process of recovery. But apart from such rather nebulous and vague good influence, many people feel, even if they would be reluctant to say, that prayer makes really no difference.

It must be confessed that very often this is quite true—prayer does make no difference, or if it makes any difference at all it is rather to make matters worse. So before proceeding to describe the conditions in which prayer for healing is effective, it may be well to clear the ground by noting some of the reasons why prayers for the recovery of health remain "unanswered."

1. Very often when we pray for invalids, especially if their sufferings are acute and dangerous, our minds are filled with the thought of their condition and not with the power of God. This kind of prayer tends rather to increase the trouble than to remove it. Real prayer consists of thinking of God. If we are thinking more of our infirmities than we are of God, we are thereby perpetuating our weakness instead of receiving His strength.

2. If we pray with anxiety, our prayers are largely frustrated. It is difficult not to be anxious for loved ones who are suffering, but anxious thoughts remaining in our minds show that we have not received the thought of God's infinite goodness and power, and that we are not rightly fixing our attention upon Him. The very fervency of our prayers may be a sign, not of faith, but of doubt and fear. We do not need to beseech and implore God to help us. It is His very nature to do so. He is always more ready to hear us than we are to pray. All we have to do is to

receive His help into our thoughts. We should continue to think of God's love in Christ until our anxiety is allayed.

3. Sometimes we pray with a divided mind. We are not quite sure whether we want our prayers answered. Much prayer is of this sort, and we need to examine our prayers critically to make sure that we are not praying at one and the same time for two results, either of which would make the other impossible. We pray, for instance, that an invalid may recover health, but at the back of our minds there lingers the thought that perhaps in some strange way his illness may be made a blessing to him, or at least a protection from even greater evils. (It is curious how such doubts as to the real benefit of health only occur when we ask it from God, and not when we call in the doctor.) Or we pray for our own health, but retain in our minds, perhaps semi-consciously, the desire for the sympathy and indulgence that ill-health affords. The result is that we "waver" instead of praying in confidence. As the Epistle says, "Let not that man think that he will receive anything of the Lord—a double-minded man, unstable in all his ways!"[1]

4. In some cases healing may be retarded or even made impossible by a subconscious resentment or fear on the part of the patient. This may have to be removed by prolonged or perhaps by expert treatment. But even such illnesses are subject to continued faithful prayer.

5. Since God is love we can only approach Him in the spirit of love and with goodwill to all men. Love is the inspiration of all true intercession. If we are harbouring in our minds suspicions and resentments, or envy and jealousy, or indulging in unreconciled quarrels and withholding forgiveness, we are thereby keeping out Love, which means that we are keeping out God. Remember what our Lord said about bringing your gift to the altar and there

[1] Jas. i. 8.

remembering that your brother has aught against you.[1] Reconciliation is a necessary prelude to worship and a condition of effective prayer.

6. In prayer we are thinking in terms of the Spirit and not of the body, even when we are praying for the relief of bodily suffering. We must remember that the material is created and controlled by the spiritual. If our minds are filled with material things and not with spiritual values our prayers lose power.

7. Frequently our thoughts for the remainder of the day contradict and deny those which we have entertained for a few minutes of prayer. When this happens our prayers lose much of their value. It must never be forgotten that our thoughts are creative, and if we contemplate disease and suffering for hours, and the healing power of God in Christ for minutes, it is the longer period of thought that is likely to prevail. Having prayed for health in the name of Christ, we must try to let our thoughts dwell on the perfect goodness and holiness of God for as long as we can during the rest of the day.

Perhaps these (and others which we shall notice later) are some of the reasons why prayer for healing has been found unavailing. It must be remembered that prayer puts into operation the laws of God's ordered universe, laws which, like others in our experience, do not operate until the necessary conditions are fulfilled. But as soon as we fulfil the conditions the laws do operate, and indeed nothing can then prevent their operation.

Take an illustration from the telephone. A few generations ago it would have seemed fantastic that distant friends should be able to speak to us almost as if they were present in the same room. But when the discoveries were made that brought the telephone into use, it was not sufficient for those who wished to avail themselves of it merely to believe that this new kind of communication was possible. It was

[1] Matt. v. 23.

necessary for the requisite conditions to be fulfilled. But as soon as these conditions were fulfilled, not only did communication become possible, but failure in communication became impossible, unless by the breaking down of the necessary conditions.

XII

PRAYER IS OBEDIENCE TO NATURAL LAW

WE must never forget that prayer is the fulfilment of law; we might say the fulfilment of natural law, for it is part of the ordered universe which God has made to be our home. Whether we think of it as natural law or supernatural law (and there is really no difference, for both are appointed by the wisdom and providence of God), we must insist both on its existence in life, and the necessity for our co-operation with it.

There are many laws or principles in life which God has made for our use, but though (like the laws of Nature) they are constantly available and ready to serve us, they cannot serve us unless we co-operate with them by fulfilling the conditions which bring them into play. It is no use our impatiently trying to make them work upon conditions of our own. We must fulfil the conditions that God has made. If we want the balloon to rise, we must fill it with something lighter than air. It is not a bit of good filling it with heavy gas and hoping for the best, or kicking it in exasperation or fervently imploring it to ascend. The simple conditions must be fulfilled.

The conditions of effective prayer are not difficult of fulfilment. As the Epistle says, "The love of God consists in fulfilling the conditions that He has laid down; and His conditions are not difficult to fulfil."[1] It is sometimes asked why, if it is God's will to heal disease, saintly people who have made a practice of prayer all their lives continue to suffer ill health. This question must be answered very reverently and with great sympathy for the sufferer.[2] But without assuming a perfect knowledge of God's will it may be suggested that

---

[1] 1 John v. 3.   [2] See also pp. 61–2.

part of the reason at least is that no matter how devout we are the laws of God's universe do not work until the requisite conditions are fulfilled. God does not yield to fervent entreaties; He gives freely to those who are prepared to take, not on their own terms, but on His.

The only difficulty in fulfilling the conditions of availing prayer lies in the simplicity of these conditions. They are made for the childlike mind. They are concerned with the things which are hid from the wise and prudent, and revealed to babes.[1] They demand patience and humility and reverence, and in this they are like the conditions which must be fulfilled by all true lovers of knowledge and all sincere scientists in whatever department of learning. In prayer we are obeying the laws which God has made for our good, and without which He never intended us to live.

But that prayer can heal disease is not happily merely a matter of opinion. It is a matter of fact and experience. The testimony is not wanting of many who have prayed in faith and found that now, as in the apostolic Church, "the prayer of faith will heal the sick."[2] It is not necessary to depend upon authority, however, or to take our belief in prayer at second hand from the experience of others. We can (and indeed in all true religion we must) test the truth in our own experience. Without taking any other person's word for it, the reader may try to see for himself what healing powers are released in prayer.

In the next chapter a simple method of prayer for healing is suggested. It is not intended to be used as a form of prayer for repetition, but as a pattern or example of the manner of prayer which will be found effective in the treatment of bodily complaints. It is not claimed that this is the only kind of prayer by which diseases are relieved. There are many ways of praying; perhaps as many as there are men and women of faith. But in all effective prayer there are some necessary elements, and these we believe are contained

---

[1] Matt. xi. 25. [2] Jas. v. 14–15.

in the simple order of prayer which is offered in the following pages.

Remember what has already been emphasised; that prayer is essentially an act of thought. We may use solemn and impressive words or symbolic and sacramental acts to help us to elevate and concentrate our thoughts. But whether we practise the laying on of hands, or anoint with oil in the name of the Lord, or use any other means of grace, the chief necessity in true prayer is to think of God and to think of Him aright. For the Christian that means to think of Him as we know Him in Christ. When we take God into our thoughts we take Him into our lives.

XIII

HOW TO PRAY FOR HEALING

BEGIN as before (p. 28) with the highest and best conception of God of which you are capable. Ability to think of God rightly ought to increase, and the more we practise prayer the more correctly, and therefore the more helpfully, we shall be able to take God into our thoughts. It is not necessary, however, to be theologically correct before beginning to pray. What is required is the thinking of the highest and purest thought of God that we can.

While thus thinking of God bring before Him in thought, and by name, the person for whom you desire the recovery of health, either yourself or some other. It is not necessary to know intimately the persons for whom we pray, and we can help in prayer people who are not known to us personally at all. Whether those we pray for are personal friends or sufferers unknown to us for whom our prayers are desired, if we have a genuine interest in them, and a real desire for their recovery and belief in its possibility, they can benefit by our prayers.

For one moment look the illness which you desire to be cured squarely in the face. We do not deny the fact of bodily disorder. It is because disorder exists that you are praying about it. You need not be afraid of it. As a disciple of Christ, you have His authority to cast out evil. Acknowledge the need. That is always the first step to its being supplied.

But do not let your mind linger on the illness or on the physical condition of the patient. Swiftly lift your mind from his needy condition to the abundant mercy of God. Having confessed the need, we may now deny that the need exists in the will and purpose of God. In God's will there is no disorder or disease. In the Heaven which is His dwelling

HOW TO PRAY FOR HEALING

place, in the unseen and eternal realm in which our spirits live, there can be no disorder or disturbance or any kind of evil whatsoever. For Heaven is the sphere of perfect life and perfect well-being. According to God's will there is no disease or sickness. Everything that God made is perfect, and no imperfection was made by Him. And what God has not created does not exist in the same sense in which exists the perfect creation of His spirit.

Dwell for a few minutes on this sphere, not far off, but pressing in closely upon us, in which God's will is done perfectly. In that Heaven—that is to say, in God's presence—there is fullness of joy and perfect peace. There is perfect order, perfect rightness and fitness; perfect adjustment to to the divine will; perfect harmony with the divine Mind; and therefore perfect health and well-being. Heaven is the realm of infinite bliss; it is the centre of a ceaseless activity for good. Heaven is another name for perfect obedience to the will of God in Christ; perfect agreement with and reconciliation to His holy will. In that unseen world there is perfect praise, as the whole host of heaven praises God continually.

Now think of God as perfect Life. He is the essence of all Being. It is by His "breath" that man becomes a living spirit.[1] With Him is the fountain of life.[2] "He giveth to all, life and breath and all things."[3] Where He is there is perfection of life and abundant well-being. His will in Christ is that we should have life, and have it abundantly. Recall what the New Testament says about life, particularly the Johannine conception of life eternal,[4] which means life of such quality or intensity that it rises above material and temporal conditions. His gift is perfect vitality and joy of living.

Remember that God is the same Spirit that dwelt in our Lord Jesus, who healed "all manner of sickness and all

[1] Gen. ii. 7.   [2] Ps. xxxvi. 9.   [3] Acts xvii. 25.
[4] John v. 24–6, xvii. 2–3.

manner of disease."[1] He is the ever living Spirit to whom "all power is given in heaven and in earth"; and Lo, He is with us alway.[2] Where that Spirit is there is forgiveness of sin and therefore destruction of its power, and therefore health and liberty and the right functioning of all our members.

Man is made in the likeness of God. That means that by the divine will we are akin in being to our Maker. The likeness of God in us has been tarnished and disfigured by sin, but in God's will we are partakers of the divine nature.[3] Man, as God made him, and as God intends him to be, is perfect. The man of God's thought, the heavenly man, and therefore the real man is a perfect being. Forget what you know of the material man, and think of his perfection in spirit as created by the Father of Spirits.

Realise that God is Mind. He is the universal Mind from which derive all our minds. It is well known that our bodies are governed and controlled by our minds, largely by that part of the mind which is subconscious. But the whole mind, conscious and subconscious, can be controlled by God, if we admit Him into our thoughts. He will "direct, control, suggest"[4] if only we allow Him to do so.

Let your thought now dwell on God as pure goodness. Where He is there can be no evil. He desires for us nothing but good. He is Himself the absolute Good, the "Good Omnipotent," to use St. Augustine's phrase. Meditate then upon the highest good, far transcending our thoughts or desires. His "answers to our prayers are ever better than our asking."[5] Remember how frequently holy Scripture calls God good, not in the sense of righteous, but just with the meaning of enjoyable, desirable, lovely. "O taste and see that the Lord is good."[6] "O give thanks unto the Lord for He is good."[7] "For the Lord is good, His mercy endureth

---

[1] Matt. iv. 23. [2] Matt. xxviii. 18–20. [3] 2 Pet. i. 4.
[4] Bishop Thomas Ken. [5] Book of Common Prayer.
[6] Ps. xxxiv. 8. [7] Ps. cxviii. 1.

for ever."[1] "O that men would praise the Lord for His goodness."[2] "I had fainted unless I had believed to see the goodness of God in the land of the living."[3]

Return to the thought that "God is love."[4] It is love that inspires us to pray, and only in the spirit of love can we pray aright. Love always "brings out the best" in us. Where love is there is liberty and joy and increased vitality. Love is the healing power, and love is the supreme power in life.

All true prayer is the acceptance of the will of God. It is the laying aside of our own will that the will of God may be accomplished in and through us. Let the mind dwell, therefore, on God's holy will. We must be careful not to think of the will of God as something less acceptable than we could desire. It is infinitely better. "Be not conformed to this world but be ye transformed by the renewing of your mind that ye may prove what is that good and acceptable and perfect will of God."[5] Think of the very best that you could wish for and then say, "Not my will but Thine be done."[6] Think of the glorious and heavenly will of God as revealed in Christ.

As our prayers should begin with adoration, they should end with thanksgiving. Thank God for all His gifts, but even more for His very being, for His presence with us and His power in us. We may conclude with some rapturous words of Scripture, such as—

> *"Bless the Lord, O my soul:*
> *And all that is within me,*
> *Bless His holy name.*
> *Bless the Lord, O my soul,*
> *And forget not all His benefits:*
> *Who forgiveth all thine iniquities;*
> *Who healeth all thy diseases."*[7]

[1] Ps. cxviii. 29.   [2] Ps. cvii. 8.   [3] Ps. xxvii. 13.   [4] 1 John iv. 8, 16.
[5] Rom. xii. 2.   [6] Luke xxii. 42; Matt. xxvi. 39.   [7] Ps. ciii.

XIV

SOME OBJECTIONS TO PRAYER FOR HEALING

BEFORE going on to consider some of the other troubles of life which may be overcome by the acceptance of God's perfect will in prayer, it may be well to attempt at this stage to answer some questions which the foregoing chapters may have raised. That the answers given here can only be brief and inadequate, need not deter us from facing frankly some of the objections which are frequently and sincerely made to the practice of prayer for healing.

1. Do you despise medical science, which surely ought to be valued as a gift of God, and the means by which in modern times God fulfils His promise in Christ of the healing of disease?

We do not despise science which is the knowledge of God in His creation, nor do we disparage the work of the medical profession. There are millions of sufferers who cannot be healed, or will not be healed, in any other way, and the merciful work of physicians and surgeons, not only in healing, but in preventing disease, and in raising the standard of public health, must be gratefully acknowledged as part of the providence of God. What we do maintain, however, is that where the requisite faith exists, disease can be healed without the use of material means, and that often in the absence of these means or where these have failed, the prayer of faith brings relief which otherwise could not be obtained.

Many physicians and surgeons recognise the importance for healing of the mentality of the patient. Prayer, in creating a right mentality of expectation and confidence, may co-operate with medical treatment in the recovery of health.

OBJECTIONS TO PRAYER FOR HEALING

In many cases in which medical science can offer no further hope of recovery, faith in the will and power of God to heal in answer to prayer has brought new life and health.

We believe therefore that faith may co-operate with medical science with the effect of greatly increasing its efficiency. But where material science is unavailable or unavailing, recourse to prayer in the manner we have suggested may result in the complete recovery of health. Where faith on the part of the patient, or of those who pray for him, is sufficient, prayer alone, without any material aid, can heal disease. But where such faith is lacking, and material aid is obtainable, it would be foolish and wrong to refuse the material means available. The rejection of material treatment could only be justified as part of an act of faith in spiritual power.

Our experience forbids us to believe that medical science is the modern equivalent of the power which our Lord imparted to His disciples, and which they exercised in the early Church. It is true that the Church did employ such simple remedies as were then known, but the whole emphasis is put on the prayer of faith, and the material remedies used are rather the ceremonial by which the prayer is accompanied.[1]

2. When you say that it is always the will of God to heal, don't you ignore the fact that it is appointed to every man to die?

Certainly this is the fact, but a distinction must be made between death and disease. The death of the body in ripe age is part of the beneficent providence of God. But is it God's will that we should pass into Eternity racked by agonising infirmity or plagued by foul diseases? In God's will death is a peaceful and triumphant passing into His fuller presence. It must always be a very solemn and momentous event, but it should not be the occasion of

[1] Jas. v. 13–18.

misery and sorrow. Saddest of all, and surely most contrary to the will of Him who has appointed for us the joyous and abundant life, is the death that is described as "a happy release." The Bible tells us of one translated in the fullness of years, whose "eye was not dim, nor his natural force abated."[1] Is not this the ideal death, and the will of God for all His children?

3. Is it right to raise hopes of recovery in the case of those who have been pronounced incurable by competent medical authority?

This objection, which is often made by those who do not themselves believe in the efficacy of prayer to heal, seems to take for granted that hopes so raised are certain of disappointment. We cannot share that view, for it is a denial alike of our faith and our experience. It would certainly be wrong to offer hope to sufferers if that hope were ill founded. To tell invalids that they can be cured merely in order to keep their spirits up, and without any reasonable belief in the possibility of their recovery, would be a deception. But when we encourage sufferers to pray for health, and pray with them for their recovery, we are sharing a Christian faith that is founded in the New Testament and in our experience of God. It is a faith, moreover, which has again and again received the blessing and authority of the Church. To tell invalids that Christ healed the sick, that He gave His disciples authority to do so, and that to our knowledge the living Christ does still heal disease to-day, is to witness to that which we know to be true. "We cannot but speak the things which we have seen and heard."[2]

There are many instances on record of invalids who have been pronounced incurable, who subsequently in response to prayer have regained their health. But in cases in which physical health has not been regained in answer to prayer the patients, far from being plunged into despair and disillusionment, are usually conscious of a spiritual blessing

[1] Deut. xxxiv. 7.   [2] Acts iv. 20.

which has uplifted them above their sufferings and given them a large measure of victory over them.

4. Do you attribute all disease to sin? If so, why do so many manifest sinners enjoy physical health while some of the most saintly people are perpetual sufferers?

To say, as we have done so decidedly, that disease is never the will of God implies that disease is the consequence of sin. We do not commit ourselves, however, to any simple and superficial view of the relation between sin and disease. Certainly disease is not due solely to the sin of the sufferer. It is, in part at least, the baneful result of the sin of all humanity. It is sometimes due particularly to the resentment, envy and ill-will and even the anxiety, not of the invalid himself, but of his immediate neighbours. Of two persons living together the resentment or fear of one may produce or aggravate a physical illness in the other.

We do believe, however, that, notwithstanding the prevalence of sin in the world, any person who opens his mind to the thought of God's healing power, and receives His perfect will in faith, is delivered from both sin and its consequences. It is not sufficient, as it is not necessary, for healing that the sufferer should be a person of saintly character. On the other hand if he devoutly believes that his sufferings are the will of God, that belief will tend to perpetuate them. It is not those who believe in God, but those who believe in the will and power of God to heal, who are healed.

Kindness and sympathy, though very precious, are not all that is required of the Christian. He must do as God tells him in the teaching of Christ. As we can see in so many other departments of life, good intentions are not enough. If we would do God's will, we must learn God's way. God's will is always for perfect health, but the conditions of healing must be fulfilled. When these simple conditions are complied with we believe that "the effectual fervent prayer of a righteous man availeth much"[1] not only in blessing

[1] Jas. v. 16.

to the spirit, but consequently in healing of the body.

People of saintly character, being more unselfish and sensitive to suffering than others, are often more seriously affected by the evil and illness in the world than others of coarser nature. For the very reason that they dwell on the suffering of the community in imaginative sympathy, they tend to reproduce it in their own persons. Kindly and tender of heart as such people are, they make the mistake of dwelling upon the evil rather than on the good. They are not to be confused with the apparently saintly people who, having a martyr complex, attract sufferings to themselves, and derive no little subconscious satisfaction from them.

5. But is not physical weakness a discipline which makes for spiritual health? Many could testify that they have grown in grace and come nearer to God as the result of an illness.

Yes, sometimes an illness by enforcing rest gives the patient leisure for thought and prayer which otherwise he would not have had, with the result that he becomes a better man. The spiritual blessing thus received, however, is due not to the physical illness but to the quiet and passivity which incidentally it has brought into the patient's life. If the person concerned had sought opportunity of reflection and meditation while in health, he might have received the same spiritual benefit, or indeed much more, without the detriment of illness, which in itself must be regarded as always an evil. It is true that God can and does bring good out of evil, but He can bring far more good out of good.

The fact that the presence of evil immediately calls out good leads some observers to suppose that evil can be the occasion or even the cause of good. As soon as anything goes wrong, God's redemptive powers rush to the rescue and are only retarded by our sinful thoughts. Thus evil may sometimes bring the forces of Good more prominently to our notice. But they are always at work and are never helped, but invariably hindered, by evil.

It is not our experience that physical infirmity or disease

makes for deeper spiritual life. On the contrary, it lowers the vitality of the sufferer, and often enfeebles the life of prayer. This hindrance to the spiritual life may be, and often is, heroically overcome by the patient, but if he attains to a higher spiritual life in spite of illness, how much more might have been accomplished in his growth in grace had he suffered no illness at all.

6. But we are plainly taught in the New Testament that it is sometimes God's will that physical infirmity should remain and not be healed. What about St. Paul's "thorn in the flesh"?

It is often assumed that St. Paul's "thorn in the flesh" was a physical illness, but this assumption requires closer examination. The figure of speech in 2 Cor. xii. 7–10 might equally well be used of other kinds of suffering. The "messenger of Satan sent to buffet" the Apostle might have been a person or persons who made his work difficult. We have all had experience of fellow workers of whose attentions or activities we would fain have been relieved, but with whom it was rather God's will that we should achieve true reconciliation.

There are other interpretations of this rather obscure passage which have the authority of great scholars. Some have thought that the thorn meant sharp attacks of temptation. More probably the allusion is to the persecution which the Apostle encountered in the course of his adventurous career.[1]

In any case, it seems hardly right to exalt this rather obscure statement of St. Paul into opposition to the plain and repeated teaching of the Gospels that our Lord healed

---

[1] Among those who interpret the "skolops" as temptation are Thomas Aquinas and Luther. Chrysostom, Theodoret and Calvin see in it an allusion to the opposition of adversaries, or of one particular opponent. If verse 10 may be taken as a commentary on the sort of "infirmities" in which the Apostle rejoices we should expect it to belong to the category of "insults, necessities, persecutions, distresses."

all manner of disease and commanded His disciples to do the same. The Apostle, it may be noted, records that he besought the Lord thrice that the "thorn" might depart. His Lord would have said that "men ought always to pray and not give up."[1]

7. But did not our Lord Himself suffer grievously? If all physical suffering is subject to the prayer of faith, why did Jesus Himself submit to bodily injury instead of averting his sufferings by faith?

Our Lord's sufferings were indeed both real and extreme. But He did not suffer from disease. He endured the persecution consequent upon His courageous attack upon the powers of evil.

This leads us to the important distinction between two kinds of suffering. One is the suffering which every Christian is called to bear; the other is that from which every Christian is promised relief. This distinction is the subject of the next chapter.

[1] Luke xviii. 1.

XV

TWO KINDS OF SUFFERING

THERE are in this life two kinds of suffering which must be carefully distinguished. For to confuse them is to misinterpret not only Scripture, but life itself.

It is quite clear that the Christian gospel calls us to suffer. "If any man will come after Me," said Jesus, "let him deny himself, and take up his cross, and follow Me."[1] Our Lord Himself suffered, and not only on Calvary. Nor were His sufferings of the spirit only, but of the body, and while still in his youth he died a violent and agonising death. Indeed, it is the suffering or Passion of Christ that the Church has down through all the centuries declared to be the source of man's salvation.

We cannot take the view that our Lord suffered so that there should be no more suffering. We are clearly bidden to follow the example of Christ, which, even if there were no explicit command of Scripture to do as He did, would make its own appeal to all who love Him. "For even hereunto were ye called: because Christ also suffered for you, leaving you an example, that you should follow His steps."[2] "Now I rejoice," says the Epistle, "in my sufferings for your sake, and fill up on my part that which is lacking of the afflictions of Christ in my flesh for His body's sake, which is the church."[3] And another Epistle declares it to be the part of the Christian "not only to believe on Him, but also to suffer for His sake."[4]

It is equally clear that the gospel offers relief from suffering. When our Lord preached in the synagogue at Nazareth, He took to Himself the prophetic announcement:

[1] Mark viii. 34; Matt. xvi. 24.
[2] 1 Pet. ii. 21.
[3] Col. i. 24.
[4] Phil. i. 29.

"The Spirit of the Lord is upon me,
 Because He hath anointed me to preach good tidings to the poor:
 He hath sent me to proclaim release to the captives,
 And recovering of sight to the blind,
 To set at liberty them that are bruised,
 To proclaim the acceptable year of the Lord."[1]

And He went on to say: "To-day hath this scripture been fulfilled." He not only healed diseases, but He taught His disciples to do so too. When the Baptist sent from prison to ask: "Art thou he that should come, or do we look for another?" our Lord replied by pointing to the relief of suffering which was so prominent a feature of His ministry. The credentials of His messiahship were to be seen in the fact that "the blind receive their sight, and the lame walk, the lepers are cleansed, and the deaf hear, and the dead are raised up, and the poor have good tidings preached to them."[2] The Christian faith calls us to a life of joy in which wants, limitations and infirmities are overcome.

Of the two kinds of suffering thus distinguished the first is incurred as a result of resistance to evil. It is the persecution consequent upon witness to the right and attack upon wrong. It is the mark of the prophet and reformer in every age, and the heritage of those who would, with all the martyrs and saints, follow Christ.

The second kind of suffering is the result, not of our resistance to evil, but of our submission to it. It consists, not of wounds received in the battle, but of the invalidism which unfits us for service.

Any particular form of suffering may belong either to the first or the second variety, and one might even pass into the other. A hurt received in the gallant endurance of persecution might later harden into a chronic injury, whether of body or soul, to which the sufferer merely submitted. We

---

[1] Luke iv. 18–19.   [2] Luke vii. 18–23.

TWO KINDS OF SUFFERING

shall not attempt any strict classification, as that must be determined by knowledge of the true nature of the suffering in each case. But disease and accident, and want and failure, fear and strife, will in general belong to the second, while all sorts of hardships, self-denials, persecutions, with calumny, betrayal and misrepresentation, will belong to the first.

While it is not possible to draw a hard-and-fast line between these two kinds of suffering, we must learn to distinguish clearly between them. To set them in contrast, let us give them somewhat emphatic names, appropriate to each in its extreme form, calling the first "Passion" and the second "Invalidism."

The features of Passion are (1) that it ought to be borne by every Christian as the normal condition of the life of faith. Those who in this world are loyal to the principles of the Gospel will suffer for it. The disciple is not above his Master, and not even in this respect can we be superior to Christ. (Though sometimes the impression is given by comfortable and popular Christians that if their Lord had only been as gracious and wise as they, He might have avoided a great deal of trouble!)

(2) It ought to be borne with joy. "Blessed are ye when men shall revile you, and persecute you, and say all manner of evil against you falsely, for My sake. Rejoice and be exceeding glad: for great is your reward in heaven: for so persecuted they the prophets which were before you."[1] It is an experience which the Christian accepts not with surprise and resentment, but with good humour and as a matter of course. Indeed, the real Christian is here in his element, and he may be said to delight in his hardships as the Apostle said that he would "glory in his infirmities,"[2] or as it is even said of our Lord that he endured the Cross "for the joy that was set before Him."[3]

This is not to suggest that our Lord's Passion was not of extreme severity, or that His sufferings were not intensely

[1] Matt. v. 10–12.   [2] 2 Cor. xii. 9–10, xi. 30.   [3] Heb. xii. 2.

real. But we must see Him in Gethsemane as on Calvary, not in the abject misery in which some schools of piety depict Him, but as a spiritual athlete engaged in a feat or exploit of faith in which the world's moral Champion passes a test of spiritual endurance and strength which leaves us breathless in reverent admiration.

Our Lord is the Man of Sorrows indeed, but not in the sense that He was perpetually sorrowful, a fiction of pious art which the Gospel narrative contradicts, but in the sense that He was able to take up the sorrows of life and bear them with that fine gaiety of spirit which is charactertistic of Him, and ought to be of all His disciples, as it has been of the greatest.

So far from ever being the cause of self-pity or complaint, Passion is to the Christian what hardship is to the athlete or sportsman, who deliberately puts difficulties in his way that he may enjoy the task of overcoming them. As the mountaineer encounters dangers and toils, and suffers exhaustion and privation and hazard for the thrill of the adventure, as the lover endures incredible hardships and performs astonishing feats and considers himself blest in his pains, so the Christian counts "it all joy when he falls into various trials."[1]

(3) Passion has redemptive value. It is that quality of vicarious suffering which bears evil in the sense of carrying it away. It is akin to the redemptive sufferings of Christ, in which evil is overcome by good. It is by taking up this sort of suffering that we "fill up that which is lacking of the afflictions of Christ,"[2] and partake of the fellowship of His sufferings.[3]

The chief features of Invalidism are (1) that it is not the normal condition of a healthy Christian life, but, on the contrary, is clearly recognised as a disorder, an illness, a disease. So far from being the element in which a healthy spirit lives it is a poisonous atmosphere in which the spirit

---

[1] Jas. i. 2.   [2] Col. i. 24.   [3] Phil. iii. 10; 1 Pet. iv. 13.

and the body alike suffer enfeeblement. It is unfitness for life.

(2) It brings no joy to any healthy mind. To take pleasure in illnesses, to "enjoy ill-health" as so many do, is rather a sign of depravity. It is right that we should have every sympathy with those who fall victims to disease, or who are compelled to live in squalor, but when the sufferer begins to cherish his misfortunes, and to take a morbid delight in them, his plight is pitiable indeed. Invalidism is not enjoyable unless by degenerates.

(3) Invalidism does no manner of good to anyone, and has no redemptive value. It has no power to make any situation better, but only worsens and aggravates trouble.

While these two kinds of suffering must be contrasted, there is one respect in which they are alike; both are subject to faith. It would be wrong to suppose that while invalidism can be relieved and overcome by faith, passion lies outside the scope of prayer. Both are to be met by faith; the difference between them is that while faith helps us to encounter and endure passion, it enables us to avoid and abolish invalidism. Passion is to be desired, and faith is the power that enables us to take up the cross and carry it. Invalidism is to be avoided, and faith is the power that delivers us from it.

Faith heals the honourable wounds of passion as it relieves the disorders of invalidism. The same faith which in Jesus healed the sick and cast out devils and raised the dead, enabled Him to perform unparalleled feats of forbearance and forgiveness, to win the supreme victory of love on the Cross, and finally to rise Himself from death.

The importance of distinguishing between these two kinds of suffering is that unless we do so we are in danger of substituting invalidism for passion. The Church, which is called to share in the passion of her Lord, so often shrinks from this divinely appointed suffering, and in doing so lapses into the invalidism which so far from honouring Christ is a disobedience to and distrust of Him.

When we shirk the suffering to which we are called in Christ we invariably take refuge, as a kind of sub-conscious "compensation," in the suffering from which Christ came to deliver us. The Christian is called "to endure hardship as a good soldier of Christ Jesus."[1] But the temptation to malinger is strong and many succumb to it. Instead of being martyrs for Christ, they become "martyrs to indigestion" or to some other bodily complaint. Instead of bearing persecution, they bear all manner of ills which are not of God's appointment but which provide them with excuse for refusing the redemptive suffering to which they are called.

[1] 2 Tim. ii. 3.

XVI

PRAYER FOR CHANGE OF CHARACTER

IT may be that the belief, as expressed in preceding chapters, that the prayer of faith avails to heal disease, has not carried the conviction of the reader. Let us turn, then, to a sphere in which there is no room for doubt that it is always God's will to answer prayer. Whatever we may think of infirmities of the body, every Christian must believe that it is invariably God's purpose and intention to heal the soul; and so we may pray with complete confidence for victory over faults of character and the abolition of sin.

Even if we were mistaken in supposing that our Lord did and does give His disciples power and authority to heal the sick, we can hardly doubt that it is the Church's function to convert the sinner, and minister to his growth in grace. Yet it is just here that the Church often fails to exercise the power that is committed to it in faithful prayer.

Instead of bringing to God in intercession the faults and failings of our neighbours in the sure faith that He will, if we allow Him, work through us to take away their sins, we are often content to make them the subject of gossip or criticism, thus only intensifying and perpetuating the sins upon which we ought rather to bring to bear the redemptive forgiveness of God. When I see a wrong and do nothing about righting it, although to do so is in my power, I become in some measure responsible for the wrong, and share the guilt of it. So when we only talk about the sins of our neighbours, or think about them, without doing anything to remove them, we put ourselves with them under condemnation.[1]

With regard to our own failings, we so often pretend that they do not exist, or that they are not so serious as they

---

[1] Is not this part of what is meant in Rom. ii. 1–3?

sometimes appear, thus refusing to take the first necessary step towards their removal; or we lapse into the defeatist attitude which says, "I'm just made like that." "I can't help it." "I've always been like that and nothing can change me."

Now, it is quite clearly the will of God that we should not remain the victims of sin. Else what did Christ die for, and what is the Christian gospel? There is nothing so certain as this, not even sin itself. "This is a faithful saying, and worthy of all acceptation, that Christ Jesus came into the world to save sinners."[1] And He saves sinners, not by taking away the consequences of their sins, but by removing the sins themselves. We "call His name Jesus because He shall save His people from their sins."[2] "Sin shall not have dominion over you"[3] is a promise upon which every Christian should lay hold with the most assured faith.

Nor must we allow our faith to be clouded by the accusation which will undoubtedly be made against it of "perfectionism." That there is a false "perfectionism" is not denied. It would confine the infinite holiness of God within the limits of human attainment. But we must assert the true perfectionism of the New Testament where our Lord enjoins us to be perfect as our Father in heaven is perfect,[4] and where the Epistle bids us "be ye holy, for I am holy."[5]

To contend that because man is a fallen creature we must remain the victims of our shortcomings and sins is to deny the gospel of redemption. In Christ we have full and complete salvation, and that means, not escape from the penalty of sin (for God does not impose penalties), but deliverance from sin itself.

Sin is essentially departure from God in thought and desire. It is rebellion against God's will, and against the blessedness that God has appointed for us. Our sins are the

[1] 1 Tim. i. 15. [2] Matt. i. 21. [3] Rom. vi. 14.
[4] Matt. v. 48. [5] 1 Pet. i. 15–16, from Lev. xi. 44.

symptoms or manifestations of this *sin*, which if we were left in it would result in spiritual death.

But God does not desire the death of a sinner, but rather that he should turn from his wickedness and live.[1] The gospel is a call to turn in desire and thought to God, to be readjusted or reconciled (to use the apostolic word) to God's perfect will. When we are so reconciled or brought into agreement with God, when our minds are brought into harmony with the divine mind, then sin (which is disagreement with God) is cleared away. It will indeed return. It will attack us again and again with renewed vehemence. But to the degree in which we are reconciled to God, to that degree we are clear of sin.[2]

We ought, therefore, to bring ourselves and our neighbours to God in earnest prayer for release from sin and for the removal of faults of character. For this purpose a form of prayer is offered in the next chapters, but the same order of meditation that has been suggested for use in prayer for bodily healing may be used for the healing of the soul, care being taken not to dwell in thought upon the faults which we wish to overcome, but upon the opposite virtues.

It is important to remember that God being perfect love, we can only approach Him with love in our hearts. Those who trust in themselves that they are righteous and despise others[3] are incompetent to pray. Love rejoiceth not in iniquity, but rejoiceth in the truth.[4] When we pray for others it must be in no spirit of criticism or self-righteousness. We may take for instruction the rule of the Epistle: "Brethren, if a man be overtaken in a fault, you who are spiritual restore such a one in a spirit of meekness; considering yourself, lest you also be tempted."[5]

When we pray for the conversion of sinners, or in other words for the transformation of our neighbours, we exercise the precious privilege that God has given us of sharing in

[1] Ezek. xxxiii. 11.   [2] See also p. 25–6.   [3] Luke xviii. 9.
[4] 1 Cor. xiii. 6.   [5] Gal. vi. 1.

His redemptive work. This is a ministry which the Church can neglect only at grave peril. If the Church should lose the power to change men morally she will therewith lose the reason of her existence. Prayer is not a substitute for faithful witness to the truth both in word and in deed, but it is the means by which the presentation of the Christian message is brought home in the gentle, unobtrusive power of the Spirit.

To regard any man as morally hopeless is to deny our gospel. Merely to put up with our neighbours' faults, even when we do so with heroic patience, is to acquiesce in evil and become "collaborationists" with sin. There is no person so depraved and fallen that God is not able to transform him. However the likeness of God in any man may be overlaid and disfigured by sin, the spiritual kinship to his Creator in which he was made can be restored. No man is beyond redemption while God lives. And redemption does not take effect in another life to come, but while it may only be carried to completion in the hereafter, it has its beginning here and now in the conversion which is a new creation and a transformation of character.

XVII

DEALING WITH OUR OWN FAULTS FIRST

BEFORE attempting to deal with the distressing faults of our neighbours and those with whom we live and work and worship, we had better give some attention to our own moral weaknesses. This is the more necessary because it is so much easier to see the faults of others than it is to notice our own. Hence our Lord's advice to all moralists, "Cast out first the beam out of thine own eye, and then shalt thou see clearly to cast out the mote out of thy brother's eye."[1]

The fact that we are imperfect ourselves does not excuse us from the duty of helping our neighbours to be better. But the best and most practical way in which we can minister to the moral health of our neighbours is first to take care of our own. The reason for this is that moral weaknesses are so infectious.

We must realise that we can easily get rid of our faults—if we want to. Our trouble is that we cling to them, and so they cling to us. But they will drop off, just as the burden dropped from the back of Christian in *The Pilgrim's Progress*, if only we go about it in the right way.

Here is an exercise in prayer that may be helpful.

Having begun with the thought of God, and while still thinking of Him to the best of our ability, we now bring *ourselves* before Him. It is only in the presence of God, that is while we hold Him in our thoughts, that we can see ourselves as we really are, and become conscious of our real need. If we have been at all successful in thinking of God we shall not now enjoy a high opinion of ourselves. Yet at the same time we shall have a new and humbling sense of our value and dignity as the objects of God's love and care.

[1] Matt. vii. 3–5.

Thoughts of our own weakness and folly and sin will now crowd into our minds. In fact, as this exercise proceeds we shall want to cry out aloud in the pain of recollection, or as some people say, we shall "feel like kicking ourselves." In particular, virtues on which we had been inclined to pride ourselves will be seen in this light for the tawdry and cheap deceptions that they are. "All our righteousnesses are as filthy rags."[1] We shall want to strip them off and bundle them away. But if our very virtues make us ashamed, how much more do our sins! Yet our sins are not the worst. They are only the ugly symptoms of *sin*, which is just dishonour.

But we must not dwell upon our sin except in so far as is necessary to make us see that it has separated us from God, and therefore from all the beauty and joy of life. The purpose of confession is not to catalogue our sins, still less is it to gaze upon them in fearful fascination, but to get rid of them. We must therefore cast them down before God, disowning and repudiating them in an act of true penitence.

To hold our sins in our thoughts, and to make them the subject of conversation, is only to perpetuate them. To be "convinced" of our sin in a sharp act of self-exposure is a very different thing from brooding over sin or becoming interested in it. There is nothing melancholic or morbid in true confession. It is an essential act of purgation, but to linger over it is as dangerous as to neglect it.

What we must do with our sins is to deny them—not in the sense of pretending that they do not exist, but in the sense of disowning, repudiating them, declaring that we want nothing more to do with them. It is not sufficient to admit the existence of our moral failure, as some people do quite cheerfully; we must acknowledge them as barriers between ourselves and God, and desire that they be cast down and destroyed.

It is not the penalty for sin, or the material consequences

[1] Isa. lxiv. 6.

of sin that we are here concerned with, but sin itself. To confess it is to recognise it as foul and shameful. So long as we cling to the thought that there is something rather nice, or funny, or clever, or romantic about it our confession is incomplete. Confession is not a good story about ourselves, nor is it an indulgence in self-portraiture. There are lepers who trade on their leprosy, and there are sinners who make a song of their sin. Nothing could be more disgusting. Confession is the act by which we come to God to have our sins abolished, as a man might go to a place of cleansing to be decontaminated.

The only way in which we can get rid of our sin is to turn from it to the goodness and love of God. We must lift our thoughts quickly from our own miserable condition to the eternal and divine forgiveness by which, and by which alone, sin is destroyed. Do not mistake the costly forgiveness of God for a sentimental indulgence which condones or excuses our sin, or pretends that we are not so bad after all. That would not be the part of love. True forgiveness takes the sin upon itself and carries it away.

We receive the forgiveness of God by taking it into our thoughts and dwelling upon it. Think of the love of God as revealed in the forgiving death of Christ. Remember that God is eternally what Jesus is historically. Take to yourself the promise of Scripture that "sin shall not have dominion over you."[1] Dwell on "the Lamb of God that taketh away the sin of the world."[2] "If we say that we have no sin we deceive ourselves and the truth is not in us; if we confess our sins, He is faithful and just to forgive us our sins and to cleanse us from all unrighteousness."[3]

Sin is absence from God, and we are absent from God when He is not in our thoughts, or when our minds are filled with that which excludes Him. Sin is essentially sin of thought, its visible symptoms being sins of word and deed. So when we return to God in thought the sin is banished.

[1] Rom. vi. 14. [2] John i. 29. [3] 1 John i. 8-9.

When we let in the light the darkness goes. When we let God in, sin goes. So now we take God into our minds, and try to hold Him in our desire.

These thoughts should be followed by a return to meditation on the righteousness of God. Let us dwell upon His holiness, and remember that we are made in His likeness, and destined by His will to be children of the Highest.

We cannot make ourselves righteous by any effort of our own, but God, our Maker, can fulfil His perfect will in us if we give our consent. "He made us and not we ourselves,"[1] and it is He who continues to make and remake us, and not we ourselves. Our part is to admit Him to that inmost mind which is the control house of our lives. "For by grace are ye saved through faith; and that not of yourselves: it is the gift of God; not of works, lest any man should boast. For we are His workmanship, created in Christ Jesus for good works which God has prepared beforehand that we should walk in them.[2] He will make us "walk in the paths of righteousness for His name's sake."[3]

We should end our confession with praise to God for His gracious power, taking care not to slip back into contemplation of our sins, or into faithless resignation to our moral weakness. If we have made our confession aright our sin is destroyed. "As far as the East is from the West so far hath He removed our transgressions from us."[4] Remember it is the sin itself, the moral weakness, the disposition to succumb to temptation, that God removes. It is not the penalty of sin that we are trying to escape (as a matter of fact there is no penalty) but the sin itself which is its own penalty. It is from sin that we are delivered in Christ and not from its remote consequences only. We "call His name Jesus for he shall save His people from their sins."[5]

It may help us to repeat some of the rapturous words of Scripture:

[1] Ps. c. 3.   [2] Eph. ii. 8–9.   [3] Ps. xxiii.
[4] Ps. ciii. 12.   [5] Matt. i. 21.

"Now unto Him that is able to keep you from falling, and to present you faultless before the presence of His glory with exceeding joy: to the only wise God our Saviour, be glory and majesty, dominion and power, both now and ever!"[1]

"Unto Him that loves us, and loosed us from our sins in His own blood, and hath made us kings and priests unto God and His Father, to Him be glory and dominion for ever and ever."[2]

"Now unto Him that is able to do exceeding abundantly above all that we ask or think, according to the power that worketh in us; unto Him be glory in the Church by Christ Jesus, throughout all ages, world without end. Amen."[3]

[1] Jude 24–5.   [2] Rev. i. 5–6.   [3] Eph. iii. 20–1.

XVIII

AN INTERCESSION FOR THE SICK OF SOUL

THINK quietly for a minute or two of the righteousness of God. God is Love, and love is the only righteousness.

Now bring before God in thought the person whom you wish to help. Mention the particular defect of character which you wish to remove. But do not allow your thought to dwell on it. Observe that such faults cannot exist in God's presence. In heaven, God's dwelling place, there is perfection only, for there God's will is fully accomplished.

Make sure that you are thinking of the person for whom you pray in a spirit of goodwill and love. His fault is, of course, culpable. You are not denying that. You must not condone the fault, or pretend that it does not exist, or does not matter. But you are not in the position of a judge, but rather of a physician. Your concern is to take away the sin, not to punish it. You must think, not of what the sinner deserves, but of what he needs.

Remember that God's way of dealing with sin is to forgive it and so help to bring the divine forgiveness to bear on the sin by a deliberate act of forgiveness on your part. Especially is this necessary if a wrong has been done to yourself. Dwell on the forgiving words of our Lord Jesus. Reaffirm the Christian belief that in His forgiveness, declaring and conveying, as it does, the eternal forgiveness of God, we have deliverance from sin.

All this time you should be thinking not so much of the person for whom you are praying as of the Person to whom you are praying. Prayer must always be centred on God, to whom alone it is addressed. It is sufficient that you associate the one for whom you pray with the thought of God in your mind. If you pray with the intention of helping someone, the effect of your prayer will be in accordance with your intention.

Where God is there can be no sin, nor any weakness or defect. For sin is absence from God. In His presence there is pure holiness. He is Himself perfect in nature. He is the Source and Maker of all strength and beauty of character. Here name the positive good feature of character which you desire to have created in the one for whom you are praying. If his fault, for instance, is impulsive anger and bad temper, dwell on the calm dignity of God's children, on the joy which is a characteristic of the Christian life, of goodwill and good-humour, of the "fruits of the Spirit," which are love, joy, peace, long-suffering, kindness, goodness, faithfulness, meekness, self-control.[1] Let your mind remain filled with these qualities of character as long as time permits.

Think of God's creative word, the convincing and converting word of truth, the word that is living and potent, sharper than a two-edged sword, piercing to the deepest recesses of our minds.[2]

Think of God as the Holy Spirit for ever pressing upon us in the gentle persistence of love. Remember that

> "*every virtue we possess,*
> *And every victory won,*
> *And every thought of holiness*
> *Are His alone.*"[3]

As before, end your prayer with thanksgiving to God as the Creator who made all men to be akin in nature to Himself. Praise God for His creative power ceaselessly active for the perfecting of our character, but permitting and requiring the co-operation of human minds in faithful prayer. Praise God for His own perfect Being, and for His eternal purpose to redeem mankind.

[1] Gal. v. 22–3.   [2] Heb. iv. 12.
[3] Harriet Auber in *The Spirit of the Psalms*.

You may find it helpful to follow this meditation by saying this prayer from the Epistle to the Colossians with the intention of helping the person or persons for whom you have been praying.

"We do not cease to pray and make request for you, that you may be filled with the knowledge of God's will in all spiritual wisdom and understanding, to walk worthily of the Lord unto all pleasing, bearing fruit in every good work, and increasing in the knowledge of God; strengthened with all power, according to the might of His glory, unto all patience and long-suffering with joy; giving thanks unto the Father who made us fit to be partakers of the inheritance of the saints in light; Who delivered us out of the power of darkness, and translated us into the kingdom of the Son of His love, in whom we have our redemption, the forgiveness of our sins, who is the image of the invisible God and the first-born of all creation."[1]

[1] Col. i. 9–15.

XIX

PRAYER FOR CHRISTIAN WORK

ALL Christians practise intercession for the work of Christ in the world. It is recognised that there are unseen, spiritual forces with which it is the function of the Church to co-operate. In pleading for prayer on behalf of the Church, we are surely on non-controversial ground.

Nevertheless, there is to be discerned in some quarters a disposition to relegate prayer to a position inferior to that given to other kinds of activity. There have been times in the history of the Church, when the clergy and other officials could justly be censured for sloth. But whatever the failings of the Church to-day, inactivity is seldom one of them. On the contrary we are almost too active. Church life is a constant round of "activities." Most Christian ministers and office-bearers are overworked. The number of committees and agencies and good causes has been multiplied almost beyond human endurance. If we are to look for a cause of the Church's weakness to-day, may it not be found in the fact that we are all too busy?

The work of the Church is to co-operate with the Holy Spirit of God. We are co-workers together with Him.[1] Our chief concern is not with our own plans and purposes, but with God's purpose. What is important is not what we are doing, but what God is doing. Our business, therefore, is to yield ourselves to God as "instruments of righteousness."[2]

The Spirit of God is ceaselessly engaged in His creative and redemptive work. But much of His work He has chosen to accomplish through men. His omnipotent love waits to be manifested in us; and through us, if we allow Him, He will fulfil His own will of perfect righteousness and perfect wisdom.

[1] 2 Cor. vi. 1; 1 Cor. iii. 9.   [2] Rom. vi. 13.

Analogies are always imperfect, but we may take as a crude illustration of this truth a house which is dark and cold. Yet there is laid on to the house an abundant current of electric power. The power is there, waiting to be revealed, but though there are lamps and radiators in every room, they are not properly in contact with the current, and therefore remain useless. Magnificent as they may be in themselves, and very ornamental, they are not fulfilling the purpose for which they were made. But now let us restore the contact and immediately the current circulates and the house is filled with warmth and light.

So it is in our work for God. Unless we are in contact with His Spirit, we are useless, with a futility that is not relieved by the feeling that we are tremendously busy. Our function is not to shine with our own brilliance, but to transmit the light that God supplies. "I am come from heaven, not to do my own will, but the will of Him that sent me."[1] The highest life is that which allows God to work through it. "Cut off from Me you can do *nothing*."[2] The last word should be emphasised.

How then are we to make the necessary contact with divine power? This is the function of prayer. But not prayer that fervently beseeches God to help us. There is no reason why God should help us. It is our duty to help God. To reverse that relation is the folly of pride. When we are so absorbed in what we are doing that we ignore what God is doing we have ceased to be His servants and are merely pleasing ourselves. When we stop working with Him, we stop working for Him.

We do not need to implore God to do His own work. He has never ceased to do it. Nor do we need to inform God of what we are doing in long catalogues of good works, with suggestions as to how best He can most usefully serve us. It is not for God to serve us; it is for us to serve God.

The kind of prayer that we need is that which puts us

[1] John vi. 38, v. 30.   [2] John xv. 5.

into contact or communion with God, and enables God to work in us to will and to do of His good pleasure. We take God into our lives when we take Him into our thoughts. We must learn, therefore, quietly and humbly to dwell in thought and desire on the infinite mercy and love of God, the omnipotent goodness that is waiting to be manifested in and through us.

This means that we must have more time for meditative prayer. We must seek release from ourselves and our own cares and ambitions so that God's will may be done in us without hindrance. We must wait upon God to see what He will have us do, and to see what He will do in us.

This is not to say that we must be wholly given up to contemplation as some saintly orders of Christian people are. There is a place in the Christian life for work, and for hard and expert work. But we do need to restore the balance of contemplation and action, to recover the rhythm of meditation and activity in which alone we can truly serve our Creator.

It was in the busy days of His ministry in Galilee, when our Lord was in such demand by the multitude that sometimes He "could not so much as eat bread"[1] that He was observed so often to retire into a quiet place to pray. We read that "He continued all night in prayer to God."[2] Even for Jesus, who could afford to do without it better than we, prayer was even more important than food or rest. The busier the day, the more time had to be found for prayer. It is in the restoration of this balance that the recovery of spiritual power lies.

We must practise the prayer that puts ourselves in God's hands in childlike trust. There is no doubt whatever that God is willing to work with us (for that is the way of His incomprehensible love) if we are willing to work with Him and in His way. But it must be with God that we work and not with the Devil, under the illusion that we are serving

[1] Mark iii. 20.   [2] Luke vi. 12.

God when we are using means that He never uses. We must frankly recognise that self-importance, and vanity and love of power, desire for preferment and praise, deceptions and harsh judgments, overbearing and guile can never serve God.

But when we sit down and relax, laying aside the weight of our own importance and the pressure of our own busyness, and try humbly to see what God is doing, and what part in His work God will give us to do, then the problems of our work will be solved as by a miracle. Hindrances are then removed, deadlocks broken, antagonisms resolved, wants supplied. And instead of our human striving there will come into our work the unseen, silent power of the Spirit which alone can accomplish the purposes of God.

XX

PRAYER FOR PROSPERITY

LET us pass now to a more controversial object of prayer and one which demands sincere and clear thinking. Many people hesitate to pray for material prosperity, fearing that such prayer must be tainted with selfishness. Religion at its best is associated not so much with wealth as with poverty. Was not our Lord Himself a poor man, and did he not proclaim the blessedness of the poor? On the other hand, Scripture contains some severe judgments of the rich, and no doubt for this reason the close association of poverty and sanctity is time-honoured in Christian sentiment.

At the same time we cannot but observe in the lives of many good people what appears to be an unresolved conflict between the acceptance of poverty and the desire for some measure of prosperity. (Perhaps in modern speech the more modest word "security" has something of the same meaning.) While cherishing a kind of pride in poverty and denouncing wealth, they nevertheless rebel inwardly against their material limitations, and secretly envy and admire those whose possessions are greater than their own. They are thus victims of the divided mind which is the enemy of true prayer.

For our real prayers are the wishes of our inmost hearts, and if in our hearts we desire wealth, yet feel that we ought to be poor, we can enjoy neither having nor not-having, and are of all men most miserable.

We must make up our minds, then, as to what degree of poverty or wealth is appropriate to the Christian life and consistent with the Christian ethic. If in the name of Christ we embrace voluntary poverty, let us do so heartily and with a single mind. But it must not be poverty that merely casts us on the charity of our friends, or the support of the community. Poverty can be as selfish in its own way as wealth. There is a poverty that is nothing better than the refusal of responsibility and which has no religious value whatever. To cast ourselves on the resources of the community is only to live on the prosperous neighbours whom we affect to despise. The harsh epithet "parasite" has often been applied to the rich; it is not always inappropriate to the poor.

The poverty that our Lord blessed and Himself practised is of a certain spiritual quality. It is the taste for simplicity and frugality of living, the capacity for self-denial, and the reverent and humble use of God's gifts. It is the rejection of avarice and covetousness and the vulgarity that prizes material above spiritual possessions; the renunciation of inordinate love of pleasure or gain or bodily comfort. To be rich in the sense of indulging the acquisitive nature and priding ourselves on luxuries which cannot be common to all, or of gratifying the lust for power and domination and display is spiritually disastrous.

At the same time, it cannot be the will of God that His children should be in want. If our Lord spoke of the blessedness of poverty, He did not thereby bless or recommend destitution. There is nothing holy in under-nourishment, whether of the body or the mind, or in bad housing with its injurious spiritual consequences, or in lives cramped and enfeebled by harassing and crippling penury.

As in regard to invalids we must speak of those who suffer want with great sympathy, yet at the same time we bring to them also a message of hope. Though God's will is hindered and thwarted in society at large, it can be done in any life to which it is admitted by faith, and we need not continue to endure that which not God's providence, but our own mean conception of it, has imposed upon us.

Our Lord taught us that we should have no anxiety about our material needs, not because material things are of no importance, or because there is any religious value in pretending that material goods make no contribution to spiritual values, but because God provides for those who trust Him—that is, for those who allow His providence to operate in their lives.

The reasoning of the sixth chapter of Matthew is not that food and clothing are unnecessary or unimportant, but that to worry about these necessaries only obstructs the processes by which God will supply them to simple trust. All life, whether in nature or in human nature, is sustained and nourished by God's care. The instinct of the birds and the inimitable beauty of the flowers give evidence of a divine Mind upon which man also is dependent for the operation of his faculties. Children grow up without effort or anxiety, provided the simple rules of life are observed. We cannot make them grow faster by worrying. Anxiety and fuss will only retard and distort the secret processes of life. Nor can we help the functioning of our own organs by anxiety, the interference of which is a potent source of mischief and malady. There are some things which we *must* learn to leave to the divine Mind if we are to live at all. Our Lord's argument is that if only we do what God has given us to do, and leave the rest to Him, we need have no want or care, for then provision for all our needs will be as simple as breathing or digestion.

What is it, then, that God has given us to do? It is to seek His rule or government in our lives, and not in our private lives only, but in the public life of the whole world. It is to put all our affairs under the control of that Spirit of Love which is the spirit of God. We do not live in a world in which the necessaries of life are normally scarce. It is the self-seeking, the avarice and fear of man that makes the scarcity. As the Elizabethan prayer puts it, "Thou, O Lord, providest enough for all men with Thy most liberal and bountiful hand: but whereas Thy gifts are, in respect of Thy goodness and free favour, made free unto all men, we (through our haughtiness and niggardliness and distrust) do make them private and peculiar."[1]

But while no one can truly desire the reign of God without working for it in the life of the community, there is a sphere within which the perfect government of God can begin at once, and that is the realm of our own personal influence. There we can either keep God out or we can let God in; but when He comes in He comes with all the perfection of His Being, and where He is there is perfect order, perfect goodness.

We must distinguish between the simple life and want. Want, like disease, is the consequence of sin, both personal and corporate.[2] It is not the will of God, but contrary to it. Wherever God's rule is admitted by faith, there God's will is done, and there God's providence operates to supply all that we need.

If we think in terms of want, we shall experience want. But when we realise that God is our Father and we His children, living in our Father's house, we can hear Him say to us as the father in the parable said to the son who was so righteous, yet so offended by his father's generosity, "Son, thou art ever with me, and all that I have is thine."[3] Or as our Lord once said: If we very imperfect parents long to give good gifts to our children, how much more will the heavenly or perfect Father give good things to those who ask Him![4]

[1] Queen Elizabeth's Prayer Book.
[2] Not necessarily, of course, the sin of the person in want.
[3] Luke xv. 31.   [4] Matt. vii. 7-11.

XXI

FAITH AND FINANCE

NOT only should we pray for complete relief from anxiety as to our own personal and domestic needs, but the material needs of the Church should also be made the subject of faithful prayer. "What soldier," asks St. Paul in this connection, "ever serves at his own expense?"[1] When we undertake work for God we do not do so out of our own resources. The anxiety that so often accompanies Christian work does no honour to Christ. If we are really engaged in His work we can trust Him to provide for it.

The extravagances and eccentricities of some who profess to live by faith have brought into discredit the habit of dependence upon prayer alone for the support of Christian work. It is not the way of faith to be improvident or self-willed, or to satisfy our own religious whims at needless expense. It is no sign of faith to be careless in the keeping of accounts, or to fail to make proper provision for those whom we employ. Faith does not release us from the ordinary obligations of good management and consideration for dependents. The finances of the Church ought not to be less carefully controlled than those of secular institutions, but more so, and the fact that some Christian organisations do not rise to the level of the best commercial honesty is a scandal and reproach.

But devout care in our stewardship of money is not inconsistent with faith in God's provision for the work which we undertake in His name. When we have examined our work prayerfully to make sure that it is sincerely done for His glory, and not our own gratification, we may go

[1] Cor. ix. 7.

forward confidently in the assurance that God will provide for it.

In this respect, too, the law of life will unfailingly operate. According to our faith, it shall be done unto us. Our thoughts and expectations will be reflected in our circumstances. If we persistently think in terms of want and insufficiency, these limitations will dominate our work. If we cherish the faith that God will supply all our needs out of His riches,[1] our faith will be confirmed and vindicated by experience.

Many of the expedients to which congregations of Christian people have recourse to raise funds for their work are as unworthy as they should be unnecessary. Christian witness is sometimes obscured by the prominence and frequency of appeals for money. If the impression is given to the public of constant financial anxiety, how can we hope to inculcate that faith in God of which the Church ought to be not only the advocate but the example?

Here, too, the emphasis has been laid far too heavily on the material, to the disparagement of the spiritual. The curious fact is that when we concentrate on material things and begin to put them first and treat them as though they were of paramount importance, then they begin to fail. Whereas when we concentrate on the spiritual, the material things seem to take care of themselves. This is just what our Lord said, "Your heavenly Father knoweth that you need all these things, but seek ye first His rule and His righteousness, and all these things shall be added unto you."[2] There is also a traditional saying of our Lord Jesus, "Seek the great things and the small things will be added to you; seek the heavenly things and earthly things will be added to you."[3]

Prayer is not a substitute for self-denial and work, which are in themselves a very effective kind of prayer, expressing as they do the sincere desire of our hearts for the cause to which we are committed. But when we have made known

[1] Phil. iv. 19.   [2] Matt. vi. 33.   [3] Quoted by Origen.

our requests to God in prayer and supplication with thanksgiving we should be anxious for nothing.[1] It is in a chapter about finance that we read, "God is able to make all grace abound toward you, so that you, always having all sufficiency in all things may abound unto every good work."[2]

[1] Phil. iv. 6.
[2] 2 Cor. ix. 8

XXII

PRAYER FOR PROTECTION

IT remains to consider one other kind of evil from which we may defend our loved ones and ourselves by prayer. There is in human affairs an element of accident which, while it greatly adds to the interest of life, is also the cause of much suffering and distress.

We never know what a day may bring forth. Despite our most careful foresight and wisest precautions, events turn out very differently from our expectations. For though (as has been repeatedly said in the foregoing pages) events tend to be of the *kind* that we expect or fear, the normal mind is unable to predict the events themselves, or to take measures adequate to prevent them.

Not only are people engaged in the rush of modern business or in dangerous employment subject to accident, but many who live a quiet and sheltered life are also its victims. A false step, or one of those natural mistakes that we all make every day, may be the cause of some mishap affecting one or more persons for life. Accident does not always inflict bodily injury. It may be a chance meeting, or the opening of a book, or the catching of a germ, or the loss of some object of material or sentimental value, or a sudden temptation, or a change in the weather.

This element of chance in life has its good side. We never know what it may bring of blessing and good fortune. There are many "lucky accidents," and not a few people can trace a lifetime of happiness to what they look back upon as a curious chance. But accidents are not always of this fortunate kind, and such happy occurrences only serve to remind us of the uncertainty of life by which we may suddenly be plunged into grief at any moment.

What parents would not wish to protect their children

from this element of accident? It is not that they want to shelter them from their due share of hardship and the rough and tumble of life, but the dangers to soul and body which lurk treacherously in the very midst of civilisation cast a shadow of anxiety over many sensitive and loving minds. If only there were some power by which our loved ones could be assured against sudden and unforseen injury!

There is! The protecting power of God is available for those who admit it into their lives by faith. The ancient wisdom of the Psalms and other Scriptures is not outworn superstition but an exalted faith, as valid for our day as for any other age.

When we look more closely at this element of accident we see that it is not after all mere chance. It is not so much just what happens, as just what must happen under certain conditions. If we knew all the circumstances instead of being surprised at its happening, we should be surprised if it did not happen. The slate which fell from the roof and would undoubtedly have brained Mr. X. if he had not at that moment put up his umbrella in response to a shower, did not fall capriciously, but precisely in accordance with the laws of God's ordered universe. The reasons why Mr. X. happened to take that road exactly at the moment at which the nail which fixed the slate had perished in the course of years sufficiently to yield up its charge to gravity, and further, the motives which caused him to take his umbrella that day contrary to his usual custom, are all buried deep in Mr. X.'s subconscious mind, but so far from Mr. X. having acted by chance, we should be bound to acknowledge, if we knew all, that he had acted strictly according to "law." As for the shower of rain that came on at that very instant, so far from that being in any sense accidental, it was the result of meteorological conditions which, if they had been completely known to us, would have convinced us that a shower at that very place and time was quite inevitable, being part of a very highly organised system and pre-arranged plan.

The fact is that the forces of Nature are meticulously governed by law. This has led some scientists to suppose that everything, including behaviour, is unalterably fixed, so that instead of man controlling nature, nature controls man. But the existence of this vast system of natural law suggests rather that nature awaits effective control by mind. If we were to discover a complicated system of machinery fitted with elaborate controls, we should conclude, not that the machinery was intended to control itself, but that it was designed to be controlled by those for whose benefit it had been created. Providence has supplied the machinery of control with the intention that the human mind, in co-operation with the divine Mind, should govern the incidents of life in accordance with the merciful and good will of the Creator.

Is not this the thought expressed in the eighth chapter of Romans, "For Nature itself is eagerly awaiting the appearance of the sons of God"? (That is, those who will in harmony with the divine Spirit co-operate with God to fulfil the real purpose of Nature.) "For Nature was left without purpose, or uncontrolled, not by its own choice (or not just by chance) but by the will of Him who made it so, in the hope that even Nature will be set free from its bondage to decay and attain the glorious liberty of the children of God."

Though no reputable scholar would now discount the record of our Lord's healing ministry as unhistorical, doubt remains with regard to the Nature miracles. Perhaps there is room for honest doubt, which is never the enemy of true religion, but care must be taken lest a cautious reserve of judgment should harden into an unscientific scepticism. There is no reason to suppose that our Lord's faith, which was able to control Nature in the case of disease, should have stopped short of the control of Nature in other respects.

When we speak of controlling Nature, what we mean is the control or adjustment of our relation to it. Perhaps it would be more accurate to speak of our obedience to Nature. When you step into your car and drive off in a direction chosen by you, or at any rate not by the car itself, you are controlling Nature by acting in accordance with its laws and in obedience to them. You are adjusting yourself to the system of natural law in such a way as to enable it to serve your need.

What we do in prayer is in part exactly what is done in driving a car or using any other device by which, through our obedience to the laws of Nature, Nature is enabled to help us. In prayer we are adjusting our minds to the vast system of natural law in such a way that natural forces come to our aid in accordance with the purpose of their Creator.

It is well known that human conduct, down to the most trifling details, is controlled by the mind, by far the greater part of which is subconscious. The choices that we make, though they seem to be quite free at the moment of choosing, are determined by suggestions received and acted upon largely without our conscious knowledge. The fact that I take one way home and not another, or that I am earlier or later than usual, may appear to be mere chance or whim, but is really decided by the subconscious faculties of the mind.

In prayer we are putting our minds under the control or suggestion of the divine Mind. We are thus admitting into our lives the Providence that is waiting to come in and direct us through our subconscious motives, in accordance with the merciful and perfectly wise will of the heavenly Father.

In praying for protection, then, we are receiving by faith the wise and loving care of God. The New Testament speaks of Providence with an assurance that far exceeds our cautious expectations. The death of a sparrow is not a matter of mere chance, but is governed by the laws of God and observed by Him. How much more are even the trifling details of our daily life under His direction. The very hairs of our heads are all numbered!

Yet Providence does not operate fully in human life until it is received and admitted by faith. It is never imposed upon us, but being the work of love, it awaits our acceptance. All spiritual gifts are of this character. They cannot be forced upon us. Truth and beauty and righteousness make their eloquent but silent appeal, and can never become fully effective in our lives until they are received. So it is with the gracious work of God's providence. We can neglect it and refuse it. But if we want it to work in our lives, and the lives of those we love, we must deliberately receive it.

XXIII

IS PRAYER SELFISH?

WHEN we begin to take prayer seriously, and the New Testament at its word, and relate prayer to the material needs which press upon us and our neighbours, and which can never be dissociated from our spiritual needs, of which they are the outward and visible sign, we immediately encounter the objection that prayer of this kind is apt to become selfish and materialistic. This objection is often made from the noblest motives, and by some of the sincerest Christians, but it is based, we believe, on a serious misunderstanding both of the demands which Christian faith makes upon us, and the help and succour which it offers.

It must be acknowledged that selfish prayer, though it may be very real and earnest, is of a low order. But we cannot regard prayer as a spiritual exercise not calculated to have material results; nor can we agree that any prayer to which an answer is expected must be selfish.

When we pray for health or protection, or the provision of material wants, we are not asking for ourselves what is not available for others on the same terms, or what we are not equally willing to ask for them if they will receive it. The desire to share in the sufferings of humanity, rather than to escape them, is prompted by the highest Christian motives, but it must find expression, not in sentiment, but in practical help and service. How then can we most effectively help the suffering community of which we are part? By adding further sufferings of our own to the common lot, or by keeping ourselves fit to bring relief to those who are in need? During an epidemic is he selfish or unsympathetic who desires to preserve his own health? Is not health just what a sick society chiefly needs? In a time of depression is he most practically helpful who sinks into gloom, adding his own sorrow to that of his neighbours', or he who maintains a spirit of hope? There is indeed a cheerfulness that jars upon sorrow in such a way as to make it all the harder to bear. We must learn to rejoice with those that rejoice and to weep with those that weep. But it is the part of true sympathy to relieve and to uplift, and not to add to the sum total of suffering under the illusion that increase of evil can do good.

We shall wish to follow in the way of Him who, though He was rich, yet for our sakes became poor, but we must remember that He did so with the express purpose that we through His poverty might be rich.[1] Whoever learns the spirit of prayer prays, not only for himself, but for others, and thus prayer, far from being selfish, becomes a blessing to many who may never be aware of the source from which a good influence pervades their lives. It may be claimed that the true worshipper is the most practically helpful person in the whole community.

It is rightly emphasised that true prayer can never be concerned solely with material benefits. Faith is the faculty by which we take God Himself into our lives, and while we believe that when God comes in He brings with Him abundant life and well-being, it is none the less God Himself and His holy will that we seek in prayer. We must not reverse our Lord's principle and seek fulfilment of our bodily wants in the hope that spiritual good will be added. If we begin by praying for spiritual health in order that we may enjoy bodily fitness, we must go on to learn to desire for its own sake that communion with God and obedience to His will which cannot fail to take effect in our circumstances as in our character. While we seek God, not for His gifts, but for His very self, we do Him no honour when we reject the gifts which accompany and reveal His presence.

One thing is so important that it must be again repeated. The condition of availing prayer is faith; but Christian faith

[1] 2 Cor. viii. 9.

is faith in the God Who is, in His own being, Love. It follows therefore that we can make little progress in prayer if we admit into our thoughts resentment or self-pity, envy or jealousy, fear or ill-will, for these and their like are the denial of the God to whom we pray. Indulgence in harsh criticism, and fault finding, or in bitter and despondent regard for our circumstances or our neighbours, or the cherished remembrance of wrongs received are the enemies of prayer.

These poisons are not easily eliminated from our natures, but when we fix our minds on God as we know Him in Christ "the fruit of the Spirit" grows within us, not of our own effort, but by the gracious work of Him who is the inspirer as He is the hearer of prayer.

It will be recognised that we have been dealing here with the elementary beginnings of prayer, and we must end as we began by insisting that true prayer, the noblest faculty with which man is endowed, is one that needs to be exercised and trained like any other, only the more earnestly. Many things have been said here briefly, and perhaps crudely, that a more scholarly treatment could have expressed in more persuasive and acceptable language, but if the reader's interest has been aroused sufficiently to lead to the study of prayer in other and more worthy books, some of which are mentioned in the list appended, the object or these pages will have been attained.

BOOK LIST

H. Anson. *Spiritual Healing* (University of London Press).
F. W. Bailes. *Your Mind Can Heal You* (Allen & Unwin).
C. W. J. Brasher, M.D. *Faith Healing* (Duckworth).
W. E. Bywater. *The Power of Thought* (Thorsons).
D. S. Cairns. *The Faith that Rebels* (S.C.M.).
F. E. Christmas (edited). *Hear My Prayer* (Hodder and Stoughton).
E. H. Cobb. *Christ Praying* (Marshall, Morgan and Scott).
Florence Converse. *The House of Prayer* (Dent).
H. E. Fosdick. *The Meaning of Prayer* (S.C.M.).
Bede Frost. *Prayer for All Christians* (Mowbray). *The Art of Mental Prayer* (Philip Allan).
L. W. Grensted. *Psychology and God* (Longmans). *This Business of Living* (S.C.M.).
Gerald Heard. *Preface to Prayer* (Cassell).
H. Hensley Henson. *Notes on Spiritual Healing* (Williams and Norgate).
E. Herman. *Creative Prayer* (James Clarke).
J. M. Hickson. *Heal the Sick* (Methuen).
Baron F. von Hugel. *Essays and Addresses*, Second Series. Chapters on "Suffering and God" and "Facts and Truths in the Life of Prayer" (Dent).
Thomas Kelly. *A Testament of Devotion* (Hodder and Stoughton).
Muriel Lester. *Ways of Praying* (Independent Press).
John Maillard. *Healing in the Name of Jesus* (Hodder and Stoughton).
G. S. Marr. *Christianity and the Cure of Disease* (Allenson).
Prentice Mulford. *Thought Forces* (Bell).
W. E. Orchard. *Prayer* (Eyre and Spottiswoode).
Mrs. Horace Porter. *Thought Faith and Healing* (Allenson).

Author of *Pro Christo et Ecclesia*. *The Christian Doctrine of Health* (Macmillan).
E. M. S. *One Thing I Know* (J. M. Watkins).
SPENCER and WORKMAN. *Spiritual Healing* (S.C.M.).
R. A. R. SPREAD. *Stretching forth Thine Hand to Heal* (Skeffington).
G. S. STEWART. *The Lower Levels of Prayer* (S.C.M.).
CANON STREETER (edited). *Concerning Prayer* (Macmillan). *The Spirit* (Macmillan).
C. TATHAM. *We the Redeemed* (Michael Joseph).
WILLIAM TEMPLE. *Essays in Christian Politics*, Chapters on "Coué and Paul" and "The Ministry of Healing" (Longmans).
EVELYN UNDERHILL. *Concerning the Inner Life* (Methuen). *Abba* (Longmans).
OLIVE WYON. *The School of Prayer* (S.C.M.).
W. P. PATERSON (edited by). *The Power of Prayer*, essays by various authors.
NORMAN GRUBB. *Touching the Invisible* (Lutterworth Press).
JIM WILSON. *Healing through the Power of Christ* (James Clarke).

Not all the above are commended in their entirety, but all contain something of special interest to the student of prayer.